CW01176481

Fit for Golf

John Stirling

General Editor Peter Verney
Medical Adviser Dr Alan Maryon-Davis
MB, Bchir, MSc, MRCP, MFCM
Medical Officer
Health Education Council

B T Batsford Ltd · London

(© *Gerald Broadhead*)

© John Stirling, Alan Maryon-Davis 1984
First published 1984

All rights reserved. No part of this publication
may be reproduced, in any form or by any means,
without permission from the Publisher

ISBN 0 7134 4117 8

Typeset by Tek-Art Ltd, Kent
and printed in Great Britain by
R J Acford
Chichester, Sussex
for the publishers
B.T. Batsford Ltd.
4 Fitzhardinge Street
London W1H 0AH

Contents

Foreword 4

Section 1 General Fitness 5

The Fitness Ethic – Fit for Sport? – Fitness Testing – Fitness Tests – The Elements of Fitness – Fitness Exercises – Exercise Sessions – Suppleness Exercises – Strength Exercises – Stamina Exercises – Circuit Training – Warming up – Warming down – Weight and Fitness

Section 2 Fit for Golf 31

Introduction – the Physical Demands of Golf – Building up Strength – Suppleness and Stamina – Exercise Circuits – Warming up before a Round – Correct Equipment – Advice for Aspiring Champions

Section 3 Ailments and Injuries 61

Introduction – Specific Injuries Associated with Golf – General Ailments and Conditions – First Aid

Index 72

Foreword

If there is one thing certain in this transient world it is that as our working days get shorter, and sometimes fewer in face of technological advance, we shall be 'burdened' by more and more leisure time. Some of us will occupy ourselves in sedentary occupations, but many more will prefer to take more and regular exercise – and this will often mean *devoting greater time and effort to sport.*

These books are not written with the beginner in mind – although he or she will find much of value in these pages – but they are rather designed for the enthusiastic amateur; the committed sportsman or sportswoman, someone who has tasted, experienced and enjoyed their sport and who wishes to improve their performance and consequently gain greater enjoyment from it.

The twin pillars of improvement in any occupation are experience and skill. Experience can only come with time and a long association with the sport, but skill in any sport is dependent on, and in many cases the product of, fitness. A general degree of fitness – physical and mental – is required in the first place to act as a foundation for the subsequent developed and specialised fitness which is needed by the enthusiast. It is the purpose of this series of books, written by acknowledged experts of great experience, to help achieve this specific fitness.

Section I of this book is devoted to the attainment of a general fitness level, albeit orientated towards sports fitness. Section II concentrates on the specific needs and related aspects – equipment, training, competition advice, etc. – of golf, and how to attain fitness in golf. Section III deals with the medical aspects of the sport – the injuries and conditions associated with golf and, finally, some First Aid principles, aimed primarily at emergencies which might occur on the golf course, but which will be of use to anyone under any circumstances.

SECTION 1
General Fitness

The Fitness Ethic

One of the most significant trends in everyday living over the past thirty years has been a growing interest in fitness. Books on general fitness abound, and most incorporate an analysis of the need for fitness, the effect of fitness on the human body and the beneficial effect when that body is fit. Although this series is designed with specific sports in mind, there is no doubt that a general degree of fitness is of inestimable value to the sportsman or sportswoman, especially as more and more people are coming into sport at a later age.

The doctors declare that there is a close link between physical fitness and mental alertness, and that a fit person, taking regular exercise, is better able to face the pace and rigours, and the emotional and physical stresses of day-to-day living. He is also more likely to sleep well and feel well. More particularly, a fit body is an efficient body.

In addition, although fitness is not a passport to health, it does make you less liable to sickness and more able to effect a speedy recovery from illness. Of great value in the field of sport is the fact that a fit person tires less easily than someone who is not, and injury in sport is often directly caused by fatigue.

The doctors will also tell you that the fit have stronger hearts, and regular exercise reduces the risk of heart disease; moreover, that lack of exercise is a major cause of heart disease, and that, if you do have a heart attack, you will have a better chance of surviving it if you are fit.

For those participating in sport, fitness gives you confidence that you won't crack up halfway, makes muscle fatigue, pulls and other injuries less likely, and gives you a competitive edge.

Fit for Sport?

Most people are fit enough for most sports and games played at a gentle pace. However, there is a basic assumption behind this series that the reader is proposing to play his sport more regularly and at a greater intensity than hitherto – in short, the committed sportsman. So certain medical warnings are necessary, and a medical check-up is advisable beforehand.

This is particularly important for anyone over 35, especially if taking up strenuous sport for the first time or after a lay-off, or for those with a history of injury or who have suffered a disability or condition which has hindered or prevented them taking regular exercise.

It is important also for those who have or have recently had a heart condition or high blood pressure, asthma or other respiratory problems, arthritis or joint trouble, especially in the back or legs.

Above all, if *you* have any doubt about the effect of regular strenuous exercise on your health, seek medical advice.

Fitness Tests

With a clean bill of medical health, or if you do not feel that a medical check-up is necessary, the next stage is to discover how fit you are.

The fitness tests described on the following pages were devised many years ago and are used as a way of finding out *progressive* levels of fitness. The essence of these tests is that if you cannot perform them without undue effort – this means without breathlessness (and the truest measure of that is whether or not you can carry out a normal conversation) you should not proceed to the next test.

For most people these tests are a formality. The tests themselves are simple, painless and speedy. For the young and healthy they hardly arouse so much as a gentle sweat; but for others – and this series of books is aimed at a broad spectrum of ages and fitness levels – some of the tests may cause severe breathlessness and discomfort. If at any time you do feel discomfort *stop*, and consult medical opinion. And, if you cannot proceed beyond a certain test, it means that your stamina is wanting and you should undertake a conditioning programme.

Fitness Test

The fitness tests listed below are in four stages of increasing difficulty. In addition, a parallel test for pulse rate is shown which specifies more exactly the relative state of your fitness. For anyone regularly engaged in sport these tests are very basic indeed, but for those who are beginning or who have been inactive for some time, they will provide a useful assessment. It is important that you should be completely healthy when carrying out these tests. If you have a cold, cough or other ailment, wait until it has subsided.

Fitness Test 1: Stairs

Walk up and down a flight of 10-15 stairs three times. (*If at any time during this exercise you feel at all uncomfortable – stop.*) At the end you should be hardly breathless and be able to carry on a normal conversation without puffing. If this is the case, proceed to fitness test 2.

Fitness Test 2: Jogging on the Spot

Making sure that you lift your feet a good 20 cm (8 in.) off the floor, run on the spot/jog on the spot for *three minutes*. (*If at any time during this exercise you feel at all uncomfortable – stop.*) Once again at the end you should be able to carry on a normal conversation. If this is the case, proceed to fitness test 3.

Fitness Test 3: Step-ups

Take a strong chair (the *second* step of the stairs used in the first test will do) – the important thing is that the rise should be not less than 35 cm (14 in.) – and step up and down (right leg up, then left leg to join it so you are standing on the chair, then left leg down, followed by right leg down, etc.). Do this briskly for *three minutes* (*two minutes* if aged over 45). (*If at any time during this exercise you feel at all uncomfortable – stop.*) You should be able to carry on a normal conversation after this test. If so, proceed to fitness test 4.

Fitness Test 4: Measured Run

Mark out a measured 1.6 km (1 mile) and then gently jog the distance. (*If at any time during this test you feel at all uncomfortable – stop.*) At the end you should be mildly breathless and your times should be as follows:

Under 45 *Men*: 10 minutes
          Women: 12 minutes
Over 45   add one minute for each span of five years

If you are slower than these times you will need to undertake further stamina-improving exercises. Otherwise, when you can perform this test without discomfort or distress, you should be fit enough to start gaining fitness for your chosen sport.

Pulse Rate Test

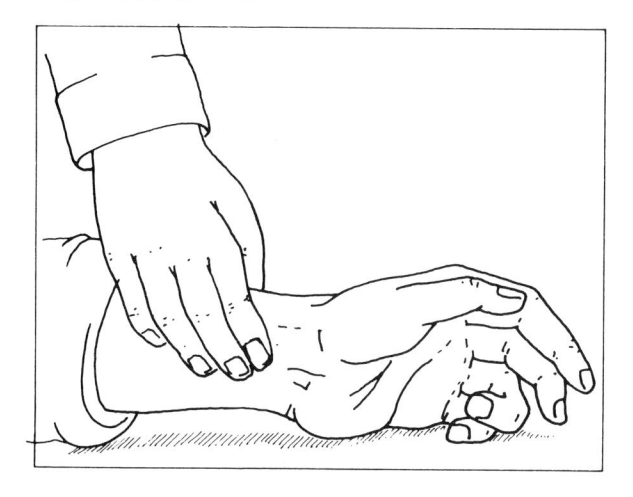

To take the pulse, first place your watch, with an easily seen second hand, where you can observe it. Then, using a pile of large books, a step or stout box – about 20 cm (8 in.) high – step up and down briskly for *three minutes*. (*If at any time you feel at all uncomfortable – stop.*) Rest for *one minute* and take your pulse for one minute. To do this, place three fingers of the right hand on the left wrist some 3 cm (1½ in.) below the mound of the thumb (*see illustration*). You should then be able to feel your pulse and count the beats. Check your rating with the table below. (The lower the pulse rate, generally the fitter you are.)

	Men	Women
Excellent	below 68	below 76
Good	68-79	76-85
Average	80-89	86-94
Below average	90-99	95-109
Very poor	100+	110+

If your score is *average* or better, you should be fit enough to start gaining fitness for your chosen sport. If it is *below average* or worse, you should undertake some further stamina-building programme.

The Elements of Fitness

There are three main elements of fitness:

suppleness
strength
stamina

and all three need to be worked on to attain general fitness. In addition, in some sports *muscle endurance, speed* and *agility* can also be important. Where applicable, exercises for these will be found in Section II.

Suppleness
(also called flexibility, or mobility)

Suppleness is the degree of movement in the joints and muscles of the body (this includes the neck, back and limbs). A gradual stiffening of the joints is a characteristic of the ageing process, and also occurs through disuse. When this happens, people are far more susceptible to strains and sprains. General suppleness is more important for some sports than others, but specific suppleness is needed in most sports, and suppleness exercises are designed to help develop the maximum range of the joints, limber up the whole body, and reduce the risk of injury.

Strength

Strength broadly means muscle power. And strength can be improved in two ways, through *isometrics* or *dynamics* (also known as isotonics).

Isometrics

Isometrics are essentially static exercises against resistance, and are intended specifically for building up muscle bulk. As such they are much used in body building, or in restoring wasted muscle after injury. They involve little or no movement and, as a result, cannot be used as stamina-improving exercises. Further, they could be dangerous for those over 35 or with high blood pressure.

Dynamics

Dynamics are exercises which do involve movement. In these, the resistance gives way and this has the effect of stretching the muscles. In addition, repetitive exercises have a strengthening effect – through alternately shortening and lengthening the muscles – and, if continued for a sufficient length of time, can also improve stamina (*see below*). Dynamics are in greater general use and have far greater application in sports fitness. Most dynamic exercises take the form of rhythmic activity, e.g. jogging, swimming, skipping.

Stamina
(also called heart and lung endurance or, sometimes, aerobics)

Stamina is essentially staying power – the ability to keep going without undue breathlessness. The muscles of the body are kept fuelled with oxygen carried in the blood stream (their waste products are also borne away in the blood stream). During strenuous exercise the muscles use oxygen at a very rapid rate, if this is not replaced quickly enough the muscles cease to function, and this is the essence of fatigue. Furthermore, the inefficient removal of waste products adds to muscle fatigue and painful exhaustion takes over. In sport, a tired person obviously cannot perform to the best of his or her ability and is also susceptible to injury. Stamina-building exercises aim to increase the efficiency of the heart and the muscles, and improve the circulation of the blood, thus rendering fatigue less likely.

Balanced Fitness

The aim of these exercises is to achieve a *balanced fitness* – extra suppleness keeping pace with improved stamina; strength married with greater flexibility – in short a programme which pays attention to all three components of fitness and exercises all the important parts of the body properly. Circuit training is the most popular way of combining these exercises, and this is discussed in more detail at the end of this section.

How you choose to regulate your exercise is up to you, for training is a matter of personal discretion and individual preference, provided that certain guidelines are adhered to and the regime is gradual and progressive.

Exercise Sessions

It is usually considered that it is necessary to carry out three sessions a week to maintain reasonable standards of fitness. Each session should last about 30 minutes in the following proportion:

20 minutes warm-up and stamina building
10 minutes split between suppleness (*two to three minutes*) and strength (*seven to eight minutes*).

Exercises should be enjoyable. If you lose motivation, *stop*, for the odds are that you will not be doing the exercises correctly to get maximum benefit from them and, if you allow your concentration to lapse, you could injure yourself.

Never exercise to the point of distress or complete breathlessness, on the other hand don't be afraid to break into a sweat. The golden rules of exercise are:
exercise conscientiously;
never to the point of distress;
never to the point of complete breathlessness;
exercise regularly;
exercise gradually, but progressively.

Suppleness Exercises

When doing these exercises it is important to stretch gradually. Push until it feels slightly uncomfortable. Hold for a second or two, then relax and repeat. For rolling exercises, rotate the part on as wide an arc as possible so that you feel you have moved over the full range.

In general, suppleness exercise sessions work systematically through all parts of the body – neck, shoulders, arms, chest, trunk, hips and legs. Repeat movements five to ten times with progressively more effort.

Spine and Hips

1 *Side Bends*

(Standing erect, with feet comfortably apart, hands at sides.)

Bend trunk to the left and at same time slide hands down the calf as far as possible keeping the back straight. Return to the upright position. Then repeat on the other side.

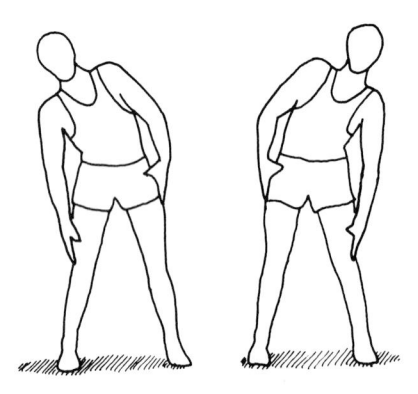

Starting repetitions: 6 each side

2 *Trunks Twists*

(Standing erect, with feet comfortably apart, hands on hips.)

Twist the trunk alternately from side to side, keeping the back as straight as possible.

Starting repetitions: 6 each side

Spine, Hips and Hamstrings

3 *Alternate Toe Touches*

(Standing erect, with feet comfortably apart, arms raised.)

Bend down and touch the opposite toe – e.g. right hand to left toe. Then return to the upright position and touch the right toe with the left hand, and so on. It is important to return to the upright position with the back straight.

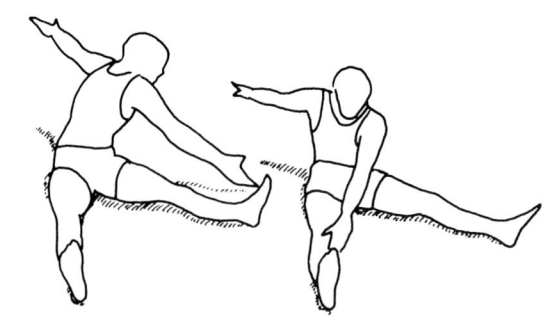

If you cannot touch the toes, reach down as far as is comfortable. As you become more supple you will find that you can reach down further and further.

Variation: carry out the exercise sitting down.
Starting repetitions: 6 each side

4 Neck Rolls

(Standing, or sitting erect [this is an exercise which can be done at any time] with feet comfortably apart, hands on hips.)

Drop chin to the chest and then slowly roll the head round reaching as far over the shoulders as is comfortable. Repeat clockwise and anti-clockwise.
Starting repetitions: 10

Shoulders

5 Shoulder Shrugs

(Standing erect, with feet comfortably apart, hands hanging loosely at the sides.)

Raise shoulders as high as you can shrug and then pull them down as far as you can.
Starting repetitions: 15

6 Wing Stretchers

(Standing erect, with feet comfortably apart, arms parallel with ground and folded as in the drawing.)

Force the elbows back as far as they will comfortably go. Count two, and relax. The body should remain upright and the head erect.
Starting repetitions: 10

Arms and Upper Body

7 Arm Circles

(Standing erect, with feet comfortably apart, arms forward at shoulder height as in the drawing.)

Bring the arms upwards brushing the ears, then around to the starting position. Flex the wrists and fingers while doing so.

Variation: hold the arms out sideways and describe small circling movements which gradually get larger until the full swing is achieved.

Practise both forwards and backwards.
Starting repetitions: 6

8 Arm Flings

(Standing, erect, with feet comfortably apart, arms held as in exercise 6, but with fingertips touching.)

Fling first the left arm out as far as it will comfortably go (keep it parallel to the ground, there is a tendency to let it droop.) Then return to the central position and repeat with the right arm. Keep the body and head erect throughout the exercise.

Starting repetitions: 10

Wrists

9 Wrist Shakes

(Standing [or sitting] erect.)

Hold out arms. Let the hands droop and then shake the wrists and hands up, down and sideways, keeping the forearm still throughout.

Starting repetitions: 15 seconds

Abdomen, Thighs and Calves

10 *The Reach*

(Standing erect, with feet comfortably apart, hands hanging loosely at the sides.)

Breathe in deeply and slowly bend backwards, at same time reach upwards with fingers outstretched. Breathe out. Hold position for 5 seconds before returning to the upright position. Breathe in deeply, then repeat.

Starting repetitions: 6

11 *The Lunge*

(Standing erect, with feet comfortably apart, and hands on hips.)

Stride sideways with the right leg pivoting the feet as in the drawing. Adopt a lunging position as in fencing. Keep pushing the right leg back, and keeping it straight at the same time, while forcing the body towards the floor. Hold for a count of 5, relax and repeat with the other leg. Keep the back straight throughout and the forward leg vertical.

Starting repetitions: 4 each side

12 *Hurdles*

(Sitting on the floor, as in the drawing, with right leg outstretched and left leg bent at right angles.)

Place hands on top of right leg and reach down towards the foot, bending the body, neck and head as close to the leg as possible (at first it will not be possible to reach very far down the extended leg, but as suppleness increases this will improve). Do not overstretch or bounce. Apply a steady pressure only, then relax. Repeat on other side.

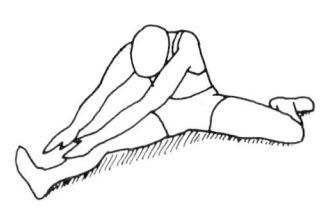

Starting repetitions: 5 each leg

15

Upper Legs

13 *Leg Swings*

(Standing erect, with feet comfortably apart, arms outstretched. For balance hold on to a chair, table or door handle.)

Swing the outer leg backwards and forwards as far as you can comfortably go. Relax and repeat on the other side.

Starting repetitions: 6 each side

14 *Knee Pulls*

(Lying flat on the ground.)

Pull first one knee, then the other – or both knees – into the chest. Hold for a count of 5, then relax and repeat. Either keep the head on the floor or bring it forward to the knee.

Variation: stand erect and lift one knee as high as you can and clasp it to the chest. Hold for a count of 5, then relax and repeat with the other leg.

Starting repetitions: 4 each leg

Lower Legs

15 *Calf Stretches*

(Standing at arm's length away from a wall, with the feet together and hands together.)

Lean forward, bending the arms and keeping the feet flat on the floor. Straighten and relax. Repeat.

Variation: this exercise can also be used to strengthen the fingers by pushing the body upright using the fingers rather than the hands.

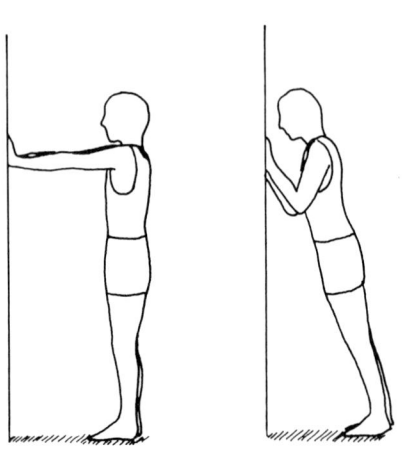

Starting repetitions: 15

Strength Exercises

These exercises are designed primarily to strengthen muscles and ligaments and, by the use of high repetition, to improve muscle endurance.

Strength exercises work on the 'overload' principle, where repetitions or resistance, or both, are gradually increased.

It is a great mistake to launch oneself into strength exercises without adequate warm-up (*see p.27*), otherwise there is a high risk of pulled muscles, etc.

The exercises below are graded by degree of difficulty

* * easy
* ** difficult
* *** very difficult

Do not attempt the most difficult until you think you can manage them comfortably.

a   **
b   Variations with stool ***
c   ***
d   Modified Push-Up (Starting position) *

Body, Arms and Shoulders

1 *Push-ups (Press-ups)*

Degree of difficulty:
Normal**
With stool***
Modified*

(Lying on the floor face downwards, feet together and hands under the shoulders.)

Push the body off the floor by straightening the arms. Then lower the body to the floor by bending the arms. It is important to keep the back straight.

Variations: try using a stool, as shown in illustrations (b) and (c), for greater strenuousness (*see star gradings*).

The modified push-up is an easier variation (see drawing [d]).

Starting repetitions: 6

Arms and Shoulders

2 *Pull-ups*

Degree of difficulty:
Normal***
Modified**

(After finding a strong bar just out of reach of the upstretched arms.)

Jump up and grasp it, either with palms facing the face or away from it, as shown. Hang for a moment, then slowly pull the body up until the chin is level with the hands. Hold, then relax and repeat. Try to avoid swaying, and keep the feet together.

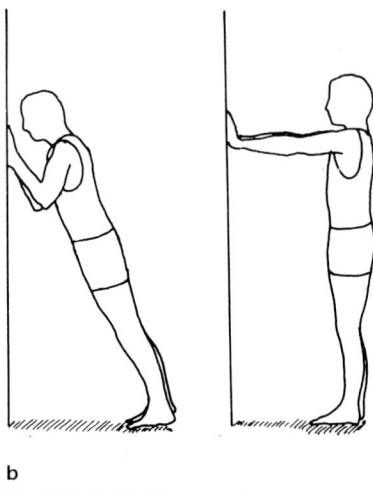

a
✶✶✶

b
Modified ✶ ✶

The modified pull-up is based on the position of suppleness exercise 15, but with the feet further from the wall, as shown in illustration (b). Push the body upright until the arms are straight, then bend the arms and allow the body to fall forward again. Using the fingers helps strengthen them. Make sure your footing is secure.
Starting repetitions: 4

3 *Hip Raises*

Degree of difficulty: *

(Sitting on the floor, with legs and feet together and hands placed flat on the ground.)

Raise the body using only the hands, until the arms are straight. Hold for a count of 5, then relax and repeat. The body should be vertical and arms completely straight when raised from the floor.
Variation: by placing a book/books under the hands the exercise can be made more difficult.
Starting repetitions: 8

Wrists and Arms

4 Broomstick Roll

Degree of difficulty: *

(Standing erect, with feet comfortably apart.)
Take a length of broomstick about 1 in. in diameter and 2 ft long, having tied a length of string to the centre point long enough to be 3-4 in. from the floor. To this is tied a weight — plastic bag of sand, a brick, a tin can holding water, etc. (start with a light weight and build up). Then, using both hands, palms down, wind the string on to the broomstick.

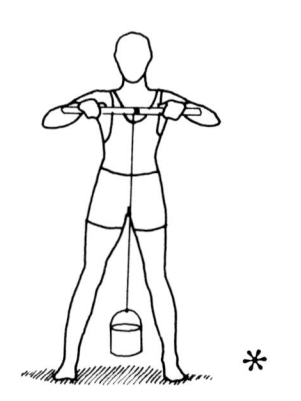

It is easier to do the exercise with the elbows bent and hands close to the chest, as in the drawing. Then carry out the exercise with the arms straight in front.

When the weight reaches the top, slowly wind it down again.

Starting repetitions: 6

5 Tennis Ball Squeeze

Degree of difficulty: *

Taking a tennis ball, two squash balls, or other rubber ball, in the hand, squeeze as hard as you can. Hold for a count of 5 seconds, relax and repeat.

Variation: hold the tennis ball in front of you, with arms straight and fingers of both hands interlocking. Squeeze the ball as hard as you can until you feel the effect in the shoulder muscles. Hold for 5 seconds, then relax and repeat.

Starting repetitions: 6

6 Fingertip Push-ups

Degree of difficulty: ***

This is an adaptation of the push-up (strength exercise 1) using the fingers rather than the flat of the hands (see illustration).

Starting repetitions: 4

***

7 Fingertip Hip Raise

Degree of difficulty: **

This is an adaptation of the hip raise (strength exercise 3) using the fingers rather than the flat of the hand.
 Starting repetitions: 6

**

Abdomen

8 *Bicycling*

Degree of difficulty: **

(Lying on the back as shown in the illustration.)
 Carry out a bicycling movement with the legs. Pull back the knee as far towards the face as comfortable then straighten it fully.
 Starting repetitions: 10 seconds

**

9 *Bent-leg Sit-ups*

Degree of difficulty:
Normal**
Variation***

(Lying on the back, legs bent and arms to the side with the feet under a low bar – wardrobe, chair or sofa – or with someone holding the ankles.)
 Raise the body *slowly* to a sitting position leaning forward, trying to touch the knees with the head. Then *slowly* return to the sitting position.

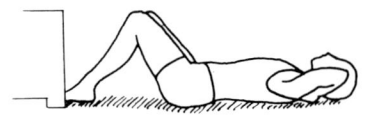

a ✳✳

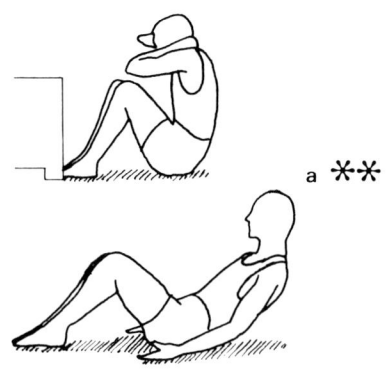

b Variation ✳✳✳

Variation: try a trunk twist at the top of the sit-up. Later, exercise without a foot support, as in illustration (b).

It is wrong to use the hands as a lever to assist or hold the position. Place the hands behind the head to remove temptation.

Starting repetitions: 4

Thighs and Legs

10 *Half Squats*

Degree of difficulty: *

(Standing erect, with feet comfortably apart, hands on hips.)

Rise on the toes and *slowly* sink down, bending the knees until the half-squat position is adopted. Hold for count of 5 seconds, then stand upright again. Relax and repeat.

Keep the body upright, the tendency is to lean forward.

Starting repetitions: 6

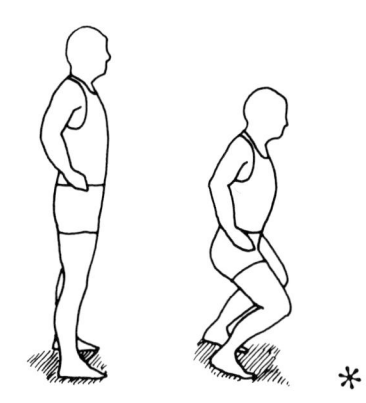

11 *Squat Thrusts (Burpees)*

*

Degree of difficulty: **

(Start as shown in illustration)

Shoot out the legs behind you into the push-up position, and then bring them forward again. Keep the feet together at all times.

Starting repetitions: 6

✳✳

12 *Sprinters*

Degree of difficulty: **

A variation on squat thrusts (burpees), but using only one leg at a time. Keep the back straight at all times.
  Starting repetitions: 6

13 *Paint Can Raises*

Degree of difficulty: *

(Sitting on a chair or bench, with thighs parallel to the ground and lower legs at right angles.)
  Take a paint can, or similar object which can be filled to the extent required to give weight, and hook it on the toe of one foot. Raise the weight *slowly* until the leg is straight, and then *slowly* lower it to the ground again. Repeat, and then change legs.
  It is important to keep the knees together. Grasping the chair will make the exercise easier to start with.
  Starting repetitions: 6

14 *Leg Raises*

Degree of difficulty:
Single *
Double **
Side *

(Lying flat on the back, with hands on the floor, palms down.)
  Raise one leg *slowly* about 9 in. then *slowly* lower it again. Relax. Repeat with the other leg.

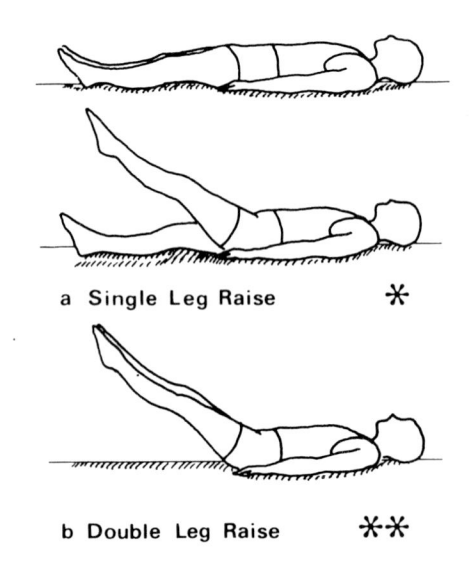

a Single Leg Raise *

b Double Leg Raise **

c Side Leg Raise   *

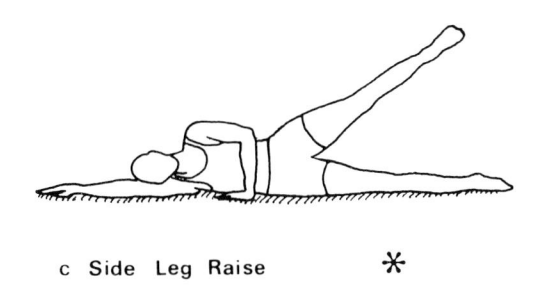

Variations: double leg raises and side leg raises, as illustrated in (b) and (c).

It is important to keep completely flat on the floor, including the head. Using the hands to help lever the legs will make the exercise easier to start with, but should be resisted as soon as possible.

Starting repetitions: 6

15 *Step-ups*

Degree of difficulty: **

(Standing erect, with hands at the sides facing the chair, stool or pile of large books 12-18 in. high.)

Place the right foot on the stool and, by using only the power of the legs, raise the body until standing on the stool. Step down again *slowly*. Repeat with the left leg. The body should remain upright throughout. There is a tendency to lurch forwards when mounting the stool. At first put the whole foot on the stool, later use only the toes.

Starting repetitions: 6

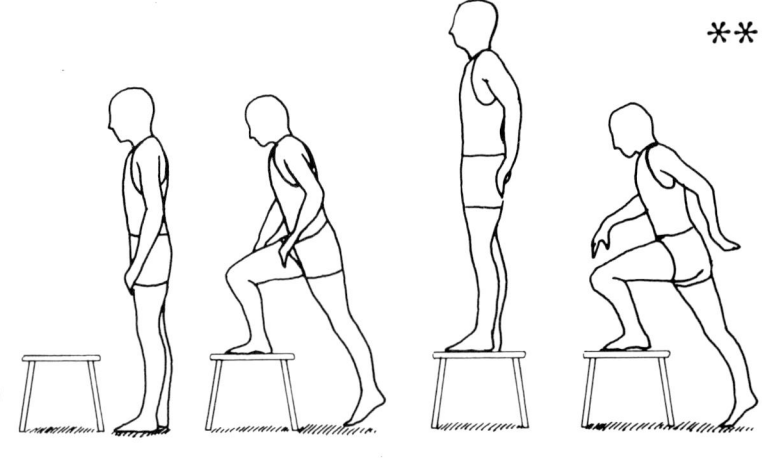

16 *Bench Jumps*

Degree of difficulty: **

(Standing alongside a bench, pile of books or bricks.)

Jump with feet together from one side to the other, and back again.

Variations: jump with feet astride, landing on the bench; hop on one leg either onto or over the bench; carry a weight, jumping on the toes rather than the whole foot, etc.

It is important to stand upright, there is a tendency to lurch either forwards or sideways. Carried out at speed, bench jumps are an excellent stamina-building exercise.

Starting repetitions: 6

Lower Legs

17 Shin Strengtheners

Degree of difficulty: *

This is a variation on paint can raises (strength exercise 13). Instead of raising the whole leg, raise only the foot, bending at the heel. It is important to raise and lower slowly. Hold at the high level for a count of 5 seconds, then lower. Repeat, then change the can to the other foot. Holding on to the bench or chair while doing the exercise is a help to start with, but should be resisted later.
Starting repetitions: 4

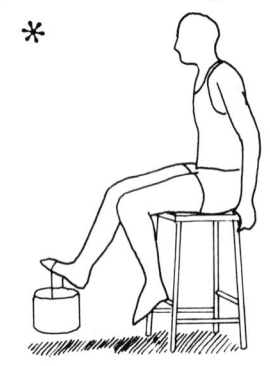

18 Calf Raises

Degree of difficulty: *

(Standing erect with arms at the sides, toes on the edge of a shallow step, or large book.)
   Bring the arms forward and at the same time rise on the toes. Lower *slowly,* relax and repeat.

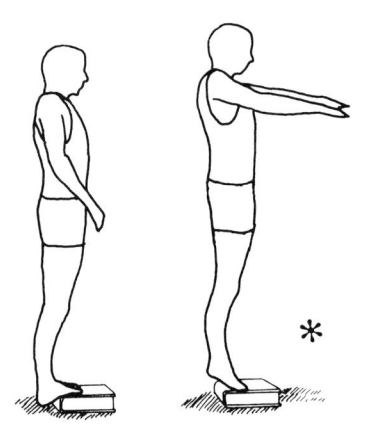

The body should remain upright throughout; there is a tendency to lean forward.
Variation: instead of rising fully on the toes, rise only halfway, and hold the position for a count of 4-5 seconds.
Starting repetitions: 6

Stamina-building Exercises

As applies for all exercises, those for stamina building should be regular – 20-minute sessions, three times a week is ideal.

Walking

Walking is probably the best way gradually to build up stamina for the unfit, the partially fit, or those who have not been taking regular exercise for some time.

This should not be just a gentle amble, but a purposeful exercise; breathing in deeply and keeping the back straight and the head up, walk briskly, lengthening the stride and the distance gradually.

Jogging

Jogging is probably the most popular form of stamina building. It is also an excellent exercise at the start of a warm-up routine (*see p.28*).

Running/Jogging on the Spot

This is a excellent exercise provided the legs are lifted high enough (30 cm [12 in.]). It is also useful for strengthening the leg muscles, particularly the hamstrings.

Skipping (rope work), bicycling and swimming are all good stamina-building exercises as are certain strength exercises if performed sufficiently vigorously at high repetition. These include:

Push-ups, modified if necessary (*Str. 1*)
Pull-ups, modified if necessary (*Str. 2*)
'Bicycling' (*Str. 8*)
Squat thrusts (Burpees) (*Str. 11*)
Step-ups (*Str. 15*)
Bench Jumps (*Str. 16*)

Build up your repetitions gradually, but make your routine progressive.

Circuit Training

Circuit training is nothing more than a range of exercises (eight to ten is usual) concentrating on different parts of the body. The mix comprises suppleness and strength exercises, so stamina building must be additional to the basic circuit, unless the circuit is done at sufficient intensity to constitute a stamina-building routine in itself. There are a number of criteria in choosing and using a training circuit:

1 The circuit should start with warm-up exercises to tone up the muscles and prevent muscle strain.
2 No two successive exercises should work on the same part of the body, thus giving variety.
3 The training programme must be progressive and comprehensive.

Within these parameters the choice is wide and

entirely personal. Three examples of circuits to help attain general fitness are listed below.

Method

First of all go through the whole circuit to familiarise yourself with the exercises — this is particularly important for the not-so-young and the not-so-fit — making sure that each exercise is carried out properly.

Having absorbed the general requirements of the circuit, you can get down to circuit training proper. Remember, never force yourself, and you should never be more than moderately breathless.

It is useful and interesting to keep a check on progress, so have a clock or watch handy. Start off by doing each circuit three times at your own speed, and then pausing for five minutes before doing another series. Time each series. The point of keeping times is to enable you to judge when you have reached a plateau in your training and the time has come for a variation. Such variation should be *gradual* and *progressive*.

The asset of circuit training is that it is possible to alter the routine in many different ways:

1 By doing the circuit faster.
2 By increasing the number of circuits before pausing.
3 By decreasing the pause time between circuits.
4 By increasing the number of repetitions within the circuit (and if you feel that you need to work on any particular weakness you can adjust accordingly); it is usual to start on a low number of repetitions and work up.

5 By adjusting the circuit at any time if it starts to become monotonous and you want a change. A further bonus is that by keeping the 'exercise content' constant within the circuit, it is possible to develop stamina by decreasing exercise time gradually.

Sample Circuits
(*starting repetitions in italics*)

Always begin with a preliminary warm-up: jog/run on spot for one minute; rest one minute; jog/run one minute.

Circuit A

Neck rolls (*Sup. 4*) (*10*)
Step-ups (*Str. 15*) (*6*)
Arm flings (*Sup. 8*) (*10*)
Calf raises (*Str. 18*) (*6*)
Bent-leg sit-ups (*Str. 9*) (*4*)
Squat thrusts (*Str. 11*) (*6*)
Shoulder shrugs (*Sup. 5*) (*15*)
Trunk twists (*Sup. 2*) (*6 each side*)
Half squats (*Str. 10*) (*6*)

Circuit B

Shoulder shrugs (*Sup. 5*) (*15*)
Bent-leg sit-ups (*Str. 9*) (*4*)
Knee pulls (*Sup. 14*) (*4 each side*)
Squat thrusts (*Str. 11*) (*6*)
Hip raises (*Str. 3*) (*8*)
Leg swings (*Sup. 13*) (*6 each leg*)
Push-ups, (modified if necessary) (*Str. 1*) (*6*)
Alternate toe-touches (*Sup. 3*) (*6 each side*)
The lunge (*Sup. 11*) (*4 each side*)

Circuit C

Side bends (*Sup. 1*) (*6 each side*)
Push-ups, (modified if necessary) (*Str. 1*) (*6*)
Leg swings (*Sup. 13*) (*6 each leg*)
Squat thrusts (*Str. 11*) (*6*)
Arm flings (*Sup. 8*) (*10*)
Bent-leg sit-ups (*Str. 9*) (*4*)
Shoulder shrugs (*Sup. 5*) (*15*)
Step-ups (*Str. 15*) (*6*)
The lunge (*Sup. 11*) (*4 each side*)

These circuits can be done at home, in the open or in a gymnasium and, if there are facilities available, make use of them (consult the resident instructor on how to incorporate them into your training circuit). But with a bit of ingenuity certain other exercises can also be done at home using everyday or easily obtainable items.

Warming-up and Warming-down

Warming-up

The purpose of warming-up, which is perhaps the single most important element in sports fitness, is twofold:

1 To tune the participant both mentally and physically.
2 To lessen the chance of injuring unprepared muscles.

With time at a premium and sports facilities expensive and in high demand, the tendency for most players is to rush into their sport at maximum power and speed. Nothing could be more calculated to lead to injury. It is essential to warm up beforehand, both physically and mentally and this pays dividends far in excess of the time expended on it. A number of players, especially if accustomed to a warmer climate, take a hot shower before play (a hot bath is too enervating) and raise the body temperature to the most favourable point for intense muscular activity. Warming the muscles relaxes them and improves muscle response; it also has the effect of stretching the muscles and making them less prone to injury if violently used. Mental warm-up is important to ease stress and tension before a match or game and generally to key the mind to the forthcoming test.

Warming-up, for the most part, consists of some jogging (running/jogging on the spot when the former is impracticable) and some simple stretching exercises – particularly of those parts of the body which are most used. Warming-up should be taken to the point of sweating, except in those sports where a lot of waiting is involved.

Method

Carry out six to ten repetitions of general stretching exercises as described on pages 11 to 16. Particularly valuable are:

Arm flings (*Sup. 8*)
Toe touches (*Sup. 3*)
Side bends (*Sup. 1*)
Trunk twists (*Sup. 2*)
The lunge (*Sup. 11*)
Arm circling (*Sup. 7*)
Calf stretch (*Sup. 15*)
Knee pulls (*Sup. 14*)
Wrist shakes (*Sup. 9*)
Neck rolls (*Sup. 4*)

Further details of warming-up exercises are given in Section II.

Warming-down

Warming-down is almost as important in the prevention of incapacitation as warming-up. Cold, damp clothes next to the skin are a prime source of chills and, for the more elderly, could lead to muscular aches. Particularly susceptible are those parts of the body where clothing has been restricted – the waist, crotch, feet, armpits and back. It is sensible after play to put on a sweater to keep the muscles warm, and to walk about after exercise carrying out a few suppleness exercises to prevent the muscles stiffening up.

The purpose of the warming-down process is to allow the body to cool down gradually. It is also sensible and hygienic to take a shower or bath as soon as you can, and to take the opportunity to massage stiff or sore muscles while they are under water. This applies particularly to the neck and shoulders. If a hot bath or shower is impracticable, a brisk rub with a towel will also help prevent irritating after-sport stiffness.

Weight and Fitness

The weight factor is as significant an element in fitness for sport as it is in general fitness. In sport, if you are overweight you are likely to be short of stamina and will tire sooner than your opponent, but in addition you will also be placing yourself at greater risk through injury. It has been shown conclusively that the more tired a sportsman or sportswoman becomes, the more prone he or she is to injury. For when fatigue strikes concentration lapses, the natural reflexes are blunted, and muscles seem no longer to be mastered by the brain.

In additon, if overweight, you expose yourself to such problems as shortness of breath, varicose veins, backache, arthritis, chest troubles, high blood pressure and diabetes (both these last two can lead to heart conditions), and other ailments and disabilities.

The table below shows a suggested weight to height ratio.

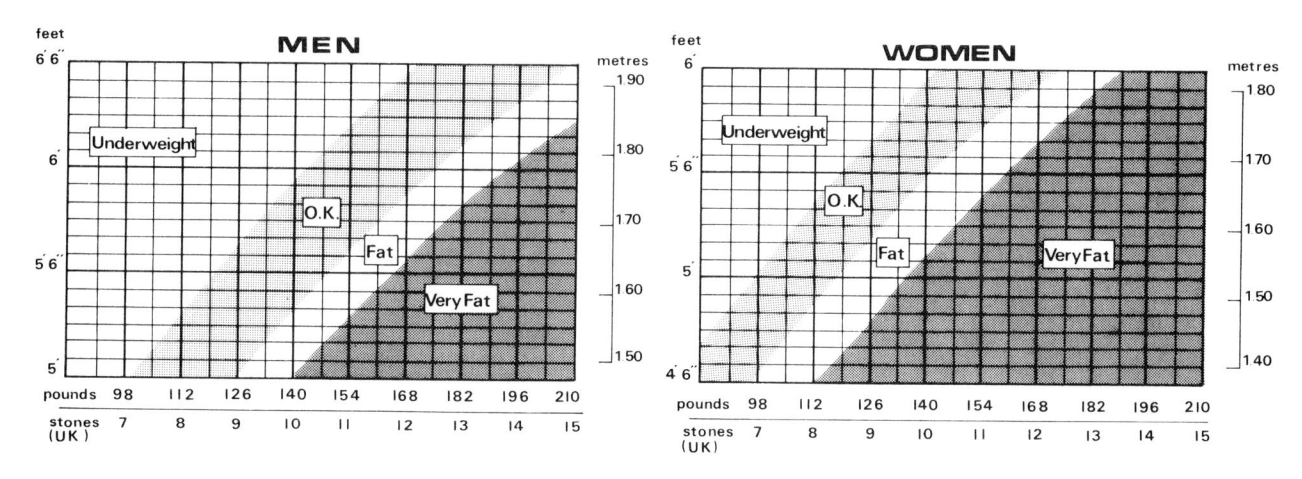

Diagram courtesy Health Education Council

SECTION 2
Fit for Golf

Introduction

Everyone knows that efficiency in sport is dependent on many factors, the most important of these being fitness, technique and equipment, which must all be of the highest standard. Golf is no exception. While this section is concerned principally with getting fit, the other two aspects are also discussed as they relate directly to staying fit and avoiding injury.

Many people will claim that playing golf regularly, probably two or three rounds a week, will in itself provide the necessary fitness. Whilst this claim is partially valid, because walking three or four miles in the fresh air several times a week must be very beneficial, this alone will never produce the high standard of fitness required for playing to one's full potential over a sustained period.

An excellent example of the value of fitness was given by the late Reginald Whitcombe, one of the three famous brothers who were outstanding players before and just after the last war. In 1937 he finished second to Henry Cotton in the Open Championship at Carnoustie.

At that time he was thirty-nine years of age and felt that he was playing the finest golf of his career, but physical tiredness, which in turn produced mental tiredness, over the last nine holes of the championship cost him the most coveted title in golf.

On his return from the championship he consulted his doctor, who gave him some excellent advice on how to achieve a higher degree of fitness. Whitcombe took his advice and the following year, at Royal St George's, Sandwich, he became the Open Champion and, at forty years of age, he was one of the oldest winners ever. He freely admitted that his fitness was the deciding factor, as the final two rounds of the championship were played at that time on one day.

Several years later I had the pleasure of playing with him in the West of England Open Championship, and when I complimented him on the excellence of his play throughout the thirty-six holes, he replied that it was mainly due to the fact that he was fitter than the majority of his contemporaries. He felt so strongly about it that he sent me a copy of the advice his doctor had given him and advised me to follow it as closely as I could. The booklet itself has long since disappeared, but the advice remains with me to this day, some 30 years later.

Another golfer who has undoubtedly been one of the best players in the world during the last twenty years, and who has benefited enormously from the fitness factor, is Gary Player. The South

African discovered very early in his career that he did not hit the ball far enough to compete against the best players in the world. He sought advice on how to increase the length of his shots. The fact that he was physically a fairly small man did not help matters, but having been advised to undergo a fairly rigorous strengthening programme, he set about it with the same intensity that characterised his whole attitude to competitive golf.

The results he obtained are positive proof of the soundness of the advice; in fact, in one of his many books, he openly admits that the extra length enabled him to win one of the world's most prestigious championships, the United States Masters, which is always played at Augusta, in Atlanta, Georgia. On his first two visits he could not reach any of the par five holes in two shots, but eventually with his newly developed strength these holes came into range and, in fact, it was his ability to obtain birdies on them that proved to be the winning factor.

Whether or not you aspire to win the Open Championship, or the United States Masters, being fit for golf is the key to success. Read the previous section of the book, which concerns fitness in general and how to attain it, and having decided to set about getting fit for golf, always remember the maxim: listen to your body; it will tell you when you are pushing it too hard. In other words, *build up gradually*.

The Physical Demands of Golf

Ever since the game began, the golf swing has always made fairly unnatural demands on the body, particularly when playing full shots. The changes in equipment and the constant search for technical perfection by the player have undoubtedly produced many present-day exponents of the game who play to a standard which forty or fifty years ago seemed quite unattainable. These players, however, are subjecting their bodies to a considerable amount of stress and strain. So let us analyse how the various elements in the golf swing affect the human frame. This will give a clear indication of the fitness requirement of golf.

Setting up to the Ball: The Tee Shot

a   Place the centre of the clubface behind the ball, with the base of the club lying naturally on the ground. The bottom front edge of the clubface should be set at right angles to the ball to target line.

Try and pick a spot two or three yards ahead of the ball on the divot scan or discoloration of the grass. There is always something on which to square the clubface.

Many players make the mistake of tilting the clubface too far forward, which in turn brings the grip too far forward. The result is that the ball will be in the incorrect place and attempts to compensate for this basic error will lead to extra, and quite unnecessary strain on wrist and elbow.

b   The hands are then placed on the club in as orthodox a manner as possible. The positioning of the hands and the amount of pressure applied to the grip are vital. The hands are the only link with the club and it is essential that they return the clubface squarely to the ball on impact.

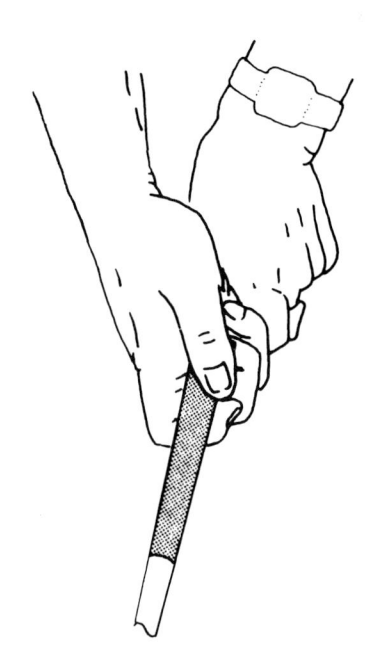

The hook grip. The right hand turns under the shaft of the club; the left hand turns the same way more on top of the shaft. The slice grip is exactly the opposite. Both hands are turned too much.

Hooking

If at the address the hands are turned too much to the right the flight of the ball will curve violently from right to left. To counteract this hooking effect most players who suffer from this malady start using an excessively fast unwinding of the lower body. *This thoroughly unnatural movement is the origin of lower back problems in many golfers.*

Solution: the solution of the hooking problem is to place the left hand on the left side of the grip (*see illustration*) with the back of the hand towards the intended target, and, consequently, the palm directly away from it. The fingers are then curled round the grip, and the pressure should be as one would use in helping a child cross the road – firm enough to control it, but not enough to hurt.

The right hand is then placed in exactly the opposite manner – back of the hand directly away from the target, palm towards it. The fingers are then curled round the grip, with the index finger slightly clear of the second finger (*see illustration*) and set as though about to pull the trigger of a gun. Once again the pressure should be firm

35

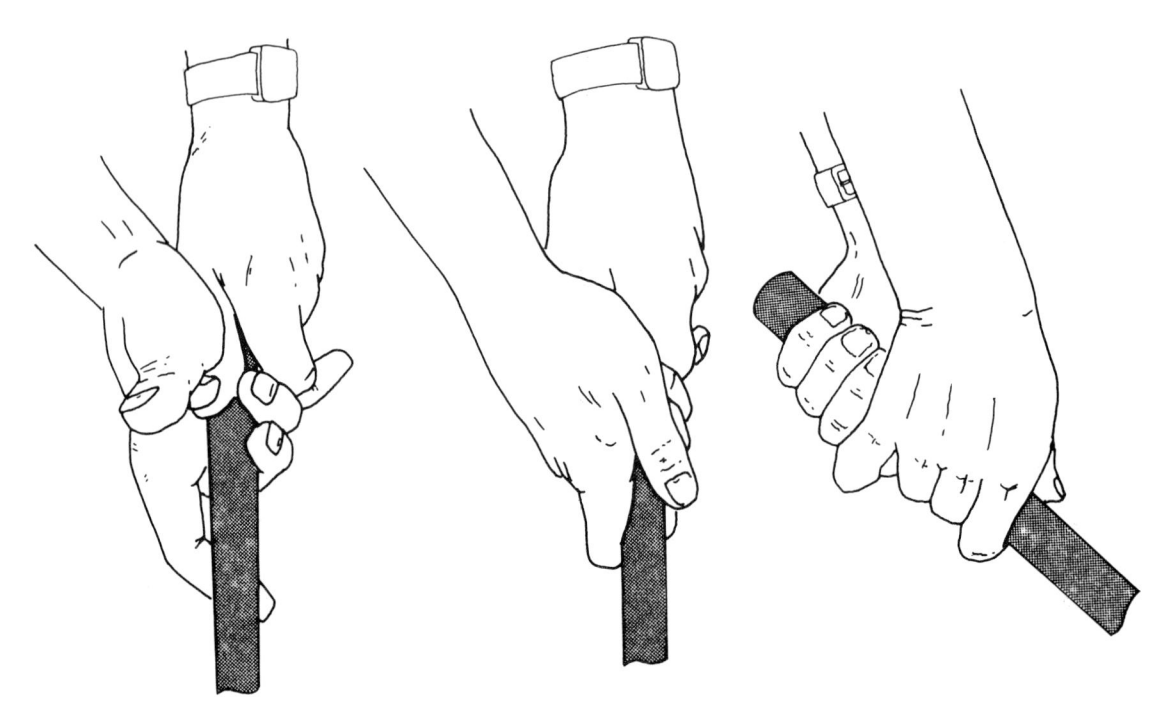

enough to control the club but sensitive enough to feel the clubhead.

The three most popular grips are the *overlapping*, in which the little finger of the right hand curls around the forefinger of the left. The *interlocking*, in which the little finger of the right hand is slipped between the forefinger and second finger of the left hand and thirdly, the *two-handed* or *baseball grip* in which all fingers are placed on the handle.

Be careful in placing the hands on the club, if they are turned too much to the right this is described as a *strong* or *hooker's grip* (see illustration). Conversely, if they are too much to the left it will be described as a *weak* or *slicer's grip*.

The correct way to assemble the overlapping grip. Always place the left hand in position first. Note the trigger position of the right index finger.

Both these grips put excessive strain on the body as it tries to compensate for the faulty clubface at impact, particularly the hooker's grip which requires an excessively fast unwinding of the lower body on the down-swing. This is the origin of a great deal of back trouble in golfers.

Apart from placement of the hands, the pressure applied is also important. An over-tight grip can lead to excessive tension in the wrists and forearms. This can lead to golfer's elbow and neck problems. A grip which is too loose tends to cause blisters.

Stance and Upper Body Alignment

With the club aimed and the hands correctly positioned on the grip, the player should measure off the correct distance from the ball. This may appear obvious, but an incorrect stance is the root cause of a great many golfers' ailments, thus it is essential to get it right from the outset.

To measure the correct distance from the ball, place the butt end of the shaft about 5-6 in. clear of a point opposite the inside of the left thigh. The left arm should be comfortably straight and, when added to the shaft length, represents the radius of the arc of the swing.

The right arm should be slightly bent at the elbow with the funny bone towards the right hip. This sets the right shoulder marginally lower than the left and rather nearer the ball. Lines drawn across the toes and shoulders should be parallel to the ball-target line (*see illustration*), and at this stage the feet should be close together.

The left foot is now moved slightly to the left until a line drawn across the back of the ball into the inside of the left heel is at right angles to the line of play (*see illustration*). The right foot is then moved to the right until the distance between the insides of both heels is roughly the same as the shoulder width.

This is crucial. If the stance is too wide the natural pivoting movement is restricted and will lead to back problems.

Posture

Correct posture is absolutely vital. The forward bending of the body which follows when the club is correctly placed on the ground behind the ball, is counterbalanced by protruding the backside slightly (*see illustration on p. 38*).

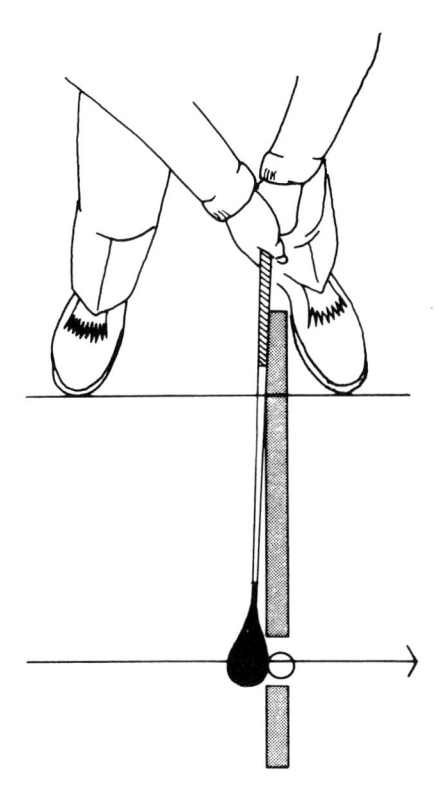

Ball position for driver. Many teachers advocate that the ball should remain in a constant position, relative to the left heel, for all shots. Others advise that the ball should be moved back towards the centre of the stance at the rate of half an inch per club. Irrespective of which system is used, the stance width should become progressively narrower as the required length of shot becomes shorter.

Note: the knees should be pressed forwards and inwards, so that they will respond to the winding and unwinding body movements during the swing. There should be a feeling of having the back perfectly straight from the top of the head to the base of the spine.

Many players are, however, so obsessed by the advice 'keep your head down' that they stick their chins on their chests at the address. *This is an extremely bad position to adopt. Apart from restricting the shoulder turn, it can lead to neck and shoulder problems.*

The Feel of the Swing

From the correct address position – and after a few pre-swing movements to break down tension (*see also warming up on p. 49*) – the player will feel ready to move the club away from the ball.

a   Push the whole club back with the left forearm keeping both wrists straight. One should feel the top end of the shaft and the bottom end move together.
b   As soon as this movement gets under way, the shoulders start turning at right angles to the upper part of the spine.
c   When the hands and clubhead approach hip height the weight and speed of the swinging clubhead will start the natural cocking of the wrists. This should be felt as an upward and inward bending which sets the shaft parallel to the ball target line when the shoulders have turned through 90 degrees. As the shoulders turn in response to the swinging arms and clubhead, the hips and left knee should turn to the right to complete the backswing sequence.

It is important that this sequence is adhered to – left shoulder, left hip and left knee all working smoothly and responding to the swinging arms and club. This will help prevent excessive strain

The correct way to line up clubhead, ball and target on one line; feet, knees, hips and shoulders parallel.

on any particular part of the body.
d   There is no exact top of the backswing, the lower body starts unwinding smoothly to the left as the arms are completing their backward journey. This initial unwinding is felt as a lateral movement of the knees and hips, which rapidly develops into a leftwards rotational movement in the hip joint. The key factor at this stage is the *maintenance of the head position*. For, if the head

moves laterally, the rotational movement of the hips will not take place at all. *Instead a lateral sliding movement of the whole body occurs, and this could put a severe amount of strain on the muscles of the right side.*

At the top of the backswing, the left arm should be comfortably straight and the right arm bent with the elbow 7-8 in. to the right of the upper chest, and pointing down.

e As the unwinding of the lower body progresses, the arms should now commence their return journey. This should be felt as a downward pulling action with the last three fingers of the left hand.

As the hands approach hip height, the wrists should start uncocking so that they are fully uncocked as the face of the club strikes squarely against the back of the ball. After impact, the clubhead should continue straight through towards the target before starting to curve inwards and upwards in the follow-through.

f At completion of the stroke, the centre of the player's body should be facing the target, with head and eyes turned to follow the flight of the ball. This is the part of the swing where the members of the 'heads-down brigade' have problems, for, in endeavouring to keep their heads firmly in their chests, the follow-through is severely impaired. *This can lead to neck and back injury and must be avoided at all costs.* A careful study of the illustrations above is strongly recommended.

Note: A useful exercise to help develop a good follow-through position is to set up to an imaginary ball and do a very short backswing before bringing the arms and club through.

Wedge Playing

Having dealt specifically with the tee shot in the previous paragraphs, the time has come to move on to another area of the game which also places considerable physical demands on the player. Namely, recovery shots from thick rough.

This is a situation allied to physical strength – as well as technique – and strong hands and forearms are a definite advantage. One has only to see the somewhat feeble efforts of some players in this situation and compare them with those of professionals or top-class amateurs. In fact, a common exercise to strengthen wrists and forearms is to scatter golf balls in thick rough and hit them out cleanly. This is an excellent strengthening exercise and helps improve clubhead speed.

Putting

This is an area of the game where physical strength is of no advantage. The main essentials are a good eye and a nice feel for distance. Both of these are natural gifts but can be developed with practice.

Short Putts

The best way to sharpen the eye for short putts is to practice from 3-4 ft to a tee stuck in the green or to another golf ball. (It is a definite advantage to have the target smaller than the diameter of the hole.)

Long Putts

To develop the feel of distance on long putts one should practise at ranges of 10-15 yd, using three or four balls. Always try to putt each ball to a different hole on the putting green.

Conclusion

It must be obvious to anyone reading the foregoing, that suppleness and good physical co-ordination are required to perform the golf swing efficiently. In particular the golfer needs:

>strong hands
>strong legs
>fluid turning and
>stamina.

Now let us assess each of these in turn.

Building up Strength, Suppleness and Stamina

Strengthening Hands

Henry Cotton, who is considered by many people to have been the greatest British-born golfer, has always stated that golf is 85 per cent hands and 15 per cent leg and body action. Not everyone would agree with the percentages, but there is no doubt that strong, well-trained hands are absolutely essential for anyone attempting to play golf to a high standard. For golf, when stripped to its barest essentials, is ball control through the medium of the hands. Cotton sums it up by saying that golf is 'brain, to hands, to clubface.'

The hands are the only contact with the club during the striking of the ball, and the manner in which they are placed on the club at address and their behaviour throughout the swing determines where the ball will go.

Wedge Writing

This is one of the finest exercises for achieving clubface control. Take a sand-iron, or wedge, and grip it correctly. The club should then be lifted to a point opposite the chest and the player should proceed to write in the air his name and address in

Write your name and address in imaginary block letters two or three times with a wedge or sand iron held in this position.

Always swing through and up to a full finish, even when swinging with the left arm only.

block letters.

Start off initially by doing this twice, until the wrists and forearms become used to it. Two or three times a week is quite sufficient and, after about a month, players should attempt to write their names and addresses four times.

This exercise does make the forearms and wrists rather tired and sore, but it is an excellent exercise. The other advantage is that every movement of the clubhead is the result of an instruction from the brain being relayed to the clubhead via the hands.

One-handed Swing

Another excellent exercise which should be done regularly, two or three times a week, is swinging one-handed with a sand-iron. The right-handed player should start off by doing twenty continuous backwards and forwards swings with the left hand. The club should then be transferred to the right hand and swung backwards and forwards ten times. Always make twice as many swings with the weaker hand; by doing this it can eventually be trained up to be as strong and effective as the master hand.

One-handed Shots

Another stage in the development of the hands and arms can now be undertaken, that is, actually hitting shots one-handed. The best club to begin with is an 8 or 9 iron; the sand-iron, or wedge, tends to be a bit heavy and can be difficult to control. It is advisable to put the ball on a low tee initially and, as the success ratio improves, the tee can be dispensed with and the ball placed on a nice lie.

Building up left arm control. Swing with a sand iron. Eventually move on to hitting balls with an eight or nine iron.

Again, the left hand and arm should be used to hit twice as many shots as the right hand and arm, in the case of a right-handed player. Twenty shots are enough to begin with and, if done two or three times a week, the player can build up to 40 after four weeks.

Two-club Practice

An invaluable exercise for strengthening hands, wrists and arms.

The completed follow-through with the two long irons. It is advantageous to swing the two or three clubs continuously.

Winding up the Bucket

This is an extremely popular exercise amongst professionals and assistant professionals. A small bucket filled with sand, or a bag filled with golf balls, is wound up and down on a piece of strong string. (This is an adaptation of the broomstick roll [*Str. 4, p. 19*].) The string should be 4-5 ft (1.2-1.5 m) in length, one end tied around the handle of the bucket and the other end threaded through a hole drilled in a piece of broom handle, about 12-14 in. (30-35 cm) in length.

Hold both arms at full stretch in front of the body at chest height and wind the bucket upwards and downwards with the piece of broom handle. The forearms will soon begin to feel sore; this must be regarded as the signal to stop. By doing this exercise at least three times a week, one can gradually build up the winding and unwinding process for a longer period before the pain appears.

The Old Tyre Exercise

On the practice ground at Penina, in Portugal's Algarve, Henry Cotton has several old car tyres available for people. The idea is to hit one of them sufficiently hard to move it, using an iron club, and by doing this regularly, Mr Cotton finds that a player's hands and arms can be trained to withstand the impact of the ball. Having tried this exercise myself, I can thoroughly recommend it and, in fact, have a tyre in my indoor teaching area at Meon Valley. However, a word of warning: it is essential to use an old club, as one could easily ruin the shaft on a good club.

It is important to do this exercise fairly gently at the outset as it puts quite a severe strain on the wrist joints and elbows.

Tennis ball Squeeze

Squeezing a tennis ball or two squash balls is another excellent way of keeping the hands in good condition. Anyone with smallish hands may find a tennis ball rather too large, in which case the squash balls would be preferable. The latter are also easier to carry around and this is a form of exercise which can be done virtually anywhere and at anytime.

Fingertip Press-ups (*Str. 6, p. 19*)

The really keen young amateur and professional golfers indulge in a considerable amount of fingertip press-ups, as a means of developing really strong hands, arms and shoulders. It is certainly a good way of doing this, but it is an exercise which should only be undertaken by people who are already reasonably strong in these departments. The ideal way to build up to doing this exercise on the floor, is to stand at arms length from a wall, the fingertips and thumb tips pressed firmly against the wall. The upper body should then move forward until the face almost touches the wall and the arms are fully bent. The arms should now straighten, pushing the upper body back to the starting position (*Str. 2, p. 18*) Ten repetitions three times a week for about six weeks are advisable before attempting this exercise on the floor.

Strengthening Legs

A good range of leg-strengthening exercises may be found on p. 21-24. However, golfers may find the following particularly useful. Bear in mind, too, that a great deal of leg exercise can be done in the comfort of one's own home, even whilst sitting in an armchair.

Leg Raise

Sitting comfortably with the back erect, raise the left leg until it is parallel to the floor. The toes should then be pointed downwards and then upwards three times in each direction, followed by three clockwise and three anti-clockwise rotations of the foot. Repeat this procedure with the right leg. Three repetitions of this exercise done three times a week will help to reduce the risk of sprained ankles, which occur quite frequently on golf courses because of the rough, uneven ground on either side of the fairways.

Chair Squat

Still using the armchair, but standing behind it and using it as a support, squatting can be practised. This will not only strengthen the legs but will make it easier to squat behind the ball when checking the line on putts. When doing this exercise for the first time, it is not advisable to let the knees bend fully, as this can sometimes cause damage. *Remember, build up gradually.*

Fluid Turning

Suppleness is one of the most essential attributes for a golfer. This, in effect, means all-round suppleness but it is especially important in the hips, shoulders, wrists and lower legs.

On p. 11-16 is a full range of suppleness exercises. However, one I find particularly useful is an adaptation of the neck roll (*Sup. 4, p.13*).

Neck Turning

An excellent way of keeping the neck muscles loose and of being less susceptible to stiff necks, is to do the following series of exercises: sit on a straight-backed chair with the spine pressed firmly against the chair, and hold the head erect with the eyes looking straight ahead. From this position, drop the head forward until the chin is resting on the chest, hold this position for three seconds and then move the head backwards as far as it will go. This position should also be held for three seconds before bringing the head back to the starting point. Now turn the head as far to the right as possible, hold the position for three seconds before returning the head to the original position, now turn fully to the left, hold for three seconds and return to the eyes front position.

From here, drop the right ear towards the right shoulder, hold for three seconds, return to the original position and drop the left ear towards the left shoulder for three seconds and return to the eyes front position.

To complete the exercise, do three clockwise neck rolls followed by three in an anti-clockwise direction. These exercises should be done three times a week. Three repetitions on each occasion are quite enough. This can lead to a much freer turn of the shoulders when swinging the golf club.

Body Suppleness Exercises

1 One of the best exercises for training the body to turn smoothly in response to the swinging

Winding a bag full of practice balls helps to develop hand and forearm strength.

Excellent for developing the suppleness required for making the correct body turn. Two or three long irons should be used for this exercise.

arms, is to place one of the long-shafted clubs across the back and hold it in position by hooking the elbows over the shaft. The body should then be set up in the same manner as it would when preparing to play a full shot with a wood. This is very important as the slight forward bending from the hips and the protruding posterior set the spine at the correct angle. This angle must be maintained throughout the turning movement. It is, in fact, one of the most important factors when trying to develop the correct body action for golf.

Having assumed the correct position, the upper body should be turned through 90 degrees to the right and then unwound through 180 degrees to the left. This position should be held for two or three seconds, with the eyes and the centre of the body facing an imaginary target, as they would be at the end of a full shot. Make sure that the heel of the right shoe has been allowed to lift, and the sole of the shoe is pointing directly away from the target.

2 The above exercise can also be done with three long irons across the back. Place the clubs so that the heads are protruding from the left side of the body in the case of a right handed person.

Again making sure that the address posture factors are applied, start the movement to the right and make it smooth and rhythmic in both directions.

Ten turns in each direction is quite sufficient to start with and these should be done three times a week for four weeks. After that 40 turns to the right and left will not prove too strenuous.

3   The above exercises can also be done indoors or out, without using golf clubs; if none are available, use a stick instead. Adopt the address posture and place the hands on the sides of the body at the hip joints and commence the smooth turning movement.

4   A fourth method of deriving the same beneficial effects as the above exercises is to fold the arms, assume the correct address position and proceed with the same turning movements.

All these exercises are extremely important as the smooth turning of the body in both directions, co-ordinated with the swinging arms, provides the golfer with power and balanced movement throughout the swing.

Building up Stamina

Any golfer today, playing at the highest level, will acknowledge that strong legs are absolutely vital. Not only for walking between shots, but to enable him to hit the ball more powerfully than the players of yesteryear. The improvement in the distance obtained is partly due to better clubs and ball technology, but also to the fact that more emphasis has been placed on leg action, particularly in the United States.

From the young, aspiring champions going through college, right up to one of the greatest players of all time, namely Arnold Palmer, now a veteran in his fifties, all indulge in a daily jogging routine. This is an excellent method of obtaining all-round fitness but should only be undertaken by people who are already reasonably fit (*see p. 25*).

There are several ways in which older golfers, who have been advised not to undertake anything as strenuous as jogging, can improve in this particular department.

1   A bit of running on the spot for one or two minutes each day will help to liven up the legs (*see p. 25*).

2   Play a few holes alone, whenever possible and walk twice as quickly as normal after each shot. This can also be done on the practice ground when collecting the balls; hit about a dozen balls, then go and collect them, moving around as briskly as possible. After a few weeks of this, the normal walking pace which other players prefer will seem very leisurely indeed.

Repairing the Damage

Although golf is prescribed by many doctors as an excellent form of exercise, there is no doubt that it can also do a certain amount of damage. Back trouble and a tendency to become round shouldered in later life are occupational hazards for professional golfers and, to a lesser degree, for amateur players. These problems can be offset by indulging in a series of contra-exercises.

1   Raise the arms to shoulder level with the elbows bent. From this position, pull both elbows back as far as possible, six times in succession.

Follow this by fully extending the arms from the elbows bent position as though making the breast-stroke in swimming. Do both these exercises, six of each movements alternately, about three times. Start off with three repetitions initially and build up to six eventually.

2   Practise swinging the club in the opposite direction fairly regularly. In other words, if you normally play right handed, swing as though you were a left hander.

Exercise Circuits

Section I (*pp. 25-27*) gives details on the conduct of an exercise circuit. Below are two possible circuits of value to the golfer:—
(Numbers in italics are for *initial* repetitions)

Circuit A
(*for the hale and hearty*)

Neck rolls (Sup. 4) (*10*)
Trunk twists (Sup. 2) (*6 each side*)
Push-ups (Str. 1) (*6*)
Leg swings (Sup. 13) (*6 each side*)
Finger tip hip raises (Str. 7) (*6*)
Step-ups (Str. 15) (*6*)
Arm circles (Sup. 7) (*6*)
Knee pulls (Sup. 14) (*4 each side*)

Circuit B
(*for older golfers*)

Neck rolls (Sup. 4) (*10*)
Wing stretchers (Sup. 6) (*6*)
Trunk twists (Sup. 2) (*6 each side*)
Half squats (Str. 10) (*6*)
Leg swings (Sup. 13) (*6 each side*)
Wrist shakes (Sup. 9) (*15 seconds*)
Arm flings (Sup. 8) (*6*)

Warming up before a Round

As in all ball games where physical movement is required, it is very important to warm up sensibly. The top tournament players and keen amateurs always arrive at the golf club at least an hour before their teeing-off time. This enables them to spend about 45 minutes warming up for the round.

On arrival at the practice ground, the player should select two new balls from his golf bag and put them in his side pockets, so that they have warmed up by the time they are required on the course. Like the player, the ball performs better when it has been warmed up.

The next thing should be to see that one has all the equipment and bric-a-brac required for the round; there must be no last minute panicking before a round.

Having checked that everything is in order, the player should take the three longest iron clubs from the bag and proceed to do the trunk turning exercise described on p. 46 for about two minutes.

The player should then take a pitching wedge, or nine iron, and play some slow rhythmic half shots, gradually building up to about ten full shots. This should be followed by moving up progressively through the alternate clubs, numbers 7, 5 and 3 irons and numbers 3 and 1 woods, not more than ten balls with each club. It is always advisable to hit the last ball off a tee with the club one intends to use off the first tee on the course, a sort of final dress rehearsal.

The player should then proceed to the putting green and select some new balls from his bag, the same type he intends using on the actual round. A few very short putts to begin with is the best way to establish confidence. The feeling of hitting the ball into the hole time after time helps to do this more quickly than anything else.

Approach putting should then be practised. This is best done by hitting several balls to different holes on the putting green, which develops touch more effectively than hitting ball after ball to the same hole.

The last few minutes of the warm-up should be employed in playing a few chip shots from the side of the putting green and a few little high pitch shots with the wedge or sand iron.

It is also advisable during a warm-up to play a few bunker shots, if there is a practice bunker available.

Quick Warm-up

Unfortunately, there are sometimes circumstances which prevent players from completing a full warm-up; lack of time, or in many cases in Britain, lack of practice facilities. In such cases, a certain amount of beneficial warming-up can still be done, starting off with the three longest irons across the back as described on p. 46, and moving on to swinging the same three clubs continuously for about a minute.

One should then take the club with which one is going to play the first tee shot and have a few swings to get the feel of swinging one club only.

Having made four or five swings, it is advisable to aim at a specific point to swing through, such as a blade of grass or a daisy head, or better still, a tee peg. This helps the player to concentrate on keeping the head steady and the eye on the object to be struck.

During the last few minutes on the tee, prior to that crucial opening shot, everyone will be feeling keyed-up to a greater or lesser extent. This can be a very uncomfortable feeling and certainly not conducive to producing a smooth rhythmic swing. The best way to alleviate this feeling of discomfort is to inhale deeply and slowly, hold the air in the lungs for a second or two then exhale slowly.

Correct Equipment

Having already stressed the need for all-round fitness and its beneficial effect on the player's performance on the golf course, it is also as well to consider equipment and clothing, which are also important aspects of the sport.

Clothing

Shoes

Good quality, leather shoes with spikes are essential, particularly during the months from late September through to late April. On exceptionally wet courses rubber shoes with spikes may be preferable.

One very important point: make sure that the shoes are wiped clean after each round or practice session, and check that the spikes are not worn down, for there is always the chance of slipping during the swing, and this can do a great deal of damage. Good spikes are essential, too, when walking downhill on wet turf. Many injuries have been caused by a fall due to faulty spikes, these injuries being either to the ankle, or to the wrist, when the player puts out a hand to save himself.

Another type of shoe which has appeared on the market in recent years has a pimpled rubber sole and this has the advantage of being a good deal lighter than the spiked leather shoe. It is also easier on the feet when the ground is very hard during summer months. Ideally, a well-equipped golfer should have a pair for winter use and one for the summer, plus a pimpled soled shoe for hard ground

It is inadvisable to try to play a full round with a new pair of shoes. Break them in gently by carrying an old comfortable pair in your golfbag and change into them at the first sign of discomfort. It is also useful to wear new shoes at practice sessions to ease them in.

Socks

The best type of socks for golf are the sports type, which are readily available in golf professionals' shops. These have cushion soles which absorb perspiration and also nullify the feeling of the spikes. It is very important to bathe one's feet after a round of golf and change into clean socks.

Trousers

When selecting golf trousers it is important to make sure that they have two back pockets. There is so much paraphenalia to be carried — tees, scorecard, pencil, pitch-mark repairer, yardage chart, spare glove, etc. — and if these items are crammed into the side pockets they stick out and tend to get in the way of the golfer who keeps the hands close to the body when putting.

For winter golf, plus-twos are more practical than trousers, which tend to get very wet and muddy at the bottom of the legs. The plus-twos also have the advantage of being warmer, and, in addition, they look much smarter than trousers tucked into socks. In fact, most private golf clubs forbid the latter mode of dress.

Upper Body Garments

These should be loose fitting for freedom of movement. In the summer months, shirts made of cotton or of a mixture which is predominantly cotton, are the best. They have much more breathability than shirts made from synthetic materials and are more absorbent. In the winter months, when it is really cold, thermal underwear, worn under a roll-neck lambswool pullover and a waterproof golf suit, will provide protection and comfort, even in the most severe conditions.

Wet-weather Clothing

When choosing waterproofs, avoid single nylon garments, as this material tends to sweat on the inside. The best material produced so far is Dartex, which is virtually waterproof and, being very soft and pliable, does not restrict the swing.

It is also important to carry other protective items when playing in wet weather: a good quality, double-ribbed golf umbrella, an all-weather glove and two small towels (one to be kept on the ribs of the umbrella, to dry the hands and grips, and the other to be kept dry in the bag and brought into use when the first one becomes soaking wet).

At the end of a round in wet conditions it is advisable to remove everything from the golf bag and wipe the heads, grips and shafts of the clubs with an old towel. Never leave wet head covers on wooden-headed clubs as the clubheads tend to absorb the moisture and will swell.

Selecting Clubs

It is always advisable to seek the advice of a golf

professional when purchasing clubs. He has the knowledge and experience to advise the prospective purchaser as to which would be the most suitable set, taking into consideration the player's age, height, size of hands, strength, etc. Many players have made the mistake of purchasing clubs from department stores or through mail order catalogues and have finished up with equipment which is totally unsuitable, and which could even cause injury in time, for most golfing ailments are cumulative.

The most important points to be considered when purchasing clubs are the *shaft flex*, the *swing weight,* the *lie of the club* and *grip thickness*. If these four factors are correct for the player, the only explanation for bad shots would be the player's faulty technique.

Shaft Flex

As a rough guide to shaft flex, a strong, young, low-handicap golfer should choose a stiff-shafted model; a higher-handicap, older golfer should go for a medium or slightly active-shafted one. A stiff shaft is very unresponsive and can cause players to force the action of the body unnecessarily. This can easily lead to lower back problems.

Swing Weight

The swing weight factor varies according to the shaft fitted to the club: stiff-shafted clubs have a slightly heavier swing weight than medium or active-shafted clubs. It is not advisable to get clubs that are too heavy as these can often lead to lower-back problems. Lighter clubs can be swung through the hitting area of the swing at a greater speed, and it is also easier to make clubs heavier than it is to lighten them. The simple process of applying strips of adhesive lead tape to the backs of the clubs increases the swing weight to any required amount. On the other hand, reducing the weight of iron clubs requires a considerable amount of buffing and filing, and with woods the soleplates have to be removed and the lead-weight bullets have to be drilled out.

Club Lie

The lie of a golf club is extremely important and the player should ensure that when he is addressing the ball correctly, the base of the club lies naturally on a firm surface, with most of the sole touching the surface.

It is acceptable to have a small gap between the toe end of the club's base and the surface on which the club is resting. If there is a large gap between the toe end or the heel end of the club and the surface, this would lead to a considerable number of off-line shots.

If the lie of the club is incorrect, the player's posture factor will tend to adapt accordingly; he will either raise or lower his wrists. This will place an unnatural strain on the body, both at address and during the swing.

Most golf professional's shops have the equipment necessary for adjusting the lie of the club to suit the player's requirements.

Grips

Grip thickness is also very important. A player with small hands should have much thinner grips than a person with large hands. A word of warning here; do not have grips that feel a bit on the thick side; it is better to have grips that feel slightly on the thin side.

If the grip is too thin there will be a tendency for the player to hold on too tightly and this can lead to golfer's elbow.

If the grip is too thick it will deaden the wrist action, which in turn places excessive strain on the body. It is also difficult to hold the club securely during the swing and this will cause blisters.

Seek your local professional's advice on the correct size of grip.

The maintenance of grips is very important. They should be scrubbed about once a month with a firm brush and hot water, into which some detergent has been added, or, if they are leather, they should be rubbed clean with a cloth dipped in methylated spirits to remove the greasy film which tends to build up on the surface. A mixture of equal quantities of castor oil and methylated spirits should then be applied to the grips with a piece of cloth and left to soak in overnight in a warm atmosphere. This helps to reproduce the soft tacky feel which makes leather grips so pleasant to use.

Advice for Aspiring Champions

Many young players nowadays are inspired by the marvellous skill and the vast amounts of money being won by players of the calibre of Nicklaus, Watson and Ballesteros. These players are constantly appearing on our television screens when the major championships are being played and they make the game appear very simple. So much so, that talented youngsters watching them are immediately tempted to think that they too could be competing at that level.

I can assure them that they would receive a rude awakening if they attempted it. My advice to anyone aspiring to become a championship-calibre golfer is to prove oneself a winner at local level before moving on to regional level, and only after winning at regional level should national tournaments be considered. Think of the champion boxers who are nursed along by their astute managers and are kept away from the really tough opposition until they have proved their worth at lower levels.

A Sound Method is Essential

Assuming that players have arrived at the situation where they feel ready to compete at the highest level, it is important to have a coach in whom one has the utmost confidence. The good coach can help to eradicate swing problems and can also give the competitor a sound knowledge of every aspect of the game. This appears to me to be one of the reasons why the top American players have the edge on players from other countries. The majority of them emerge from colleges which employ first class coaches and the young players whom they coach have a sound working knowledge of the mechanics of the golf swing by the time they are ready to compete in major tournaments.

Practise Constructively

The main areas to concentrate on when practising are putting, chipping, pitching and driving, in that order. In a two-hour practice session, the time should be broken up thus: one hour putting, half an hour chipping and pitching and the other half hour should be devoted to driving; and don't forget to have a decent warm-up before you start.

Always practise to a target, and think before hitting each shot that it is a crucial shot in a tournament. Try and simulate pressure situations, so that when they really do arise the player will feel that it is a regular occurrence and can be coped with. Gary Player was a great believer in this and freely admits that he stood over thousands of practice putts and bunker shots, saying to himself: 'this for the championship'.

Check Your Equipment

Before setting off for a tournament, check that the grips on the clubs are in good condition – slippery grips can produce poorly hit shots. See that the heads on the wooden clubs are not loose and that the neck whippings are in good condition. Make sure that the waterproof clothing and umbrella are one hundred per cent effective. Check that the shoe spikes are not worn down and don't take brand new shoes to a tournament. The same applies to golf gloves – break them in a little so that they feel snug and comfortable. The best way is to have a checklist and run through it item by item before setting off for the tournament venue.

Playing a Practice Round

In order to give oneself the best chance of success, it is essential to have at least one practice round on a strange course. This should be played in a sensible, thoughtful manner so that the player can get a good assessment of the most important factors. These are: the pace of the greens, the texture of the sand in the bunkers, the out-of-bounds areas and other trouble spots to be avoided at all costs.

Never play for a score in a practice round, just take a good look at the course and make a note of the above factors.

Nowadays many courses have a yardage chart which can be purchased in the professionals' shop. This can be most helpful with club selection and, in my opinion, is a must.

On the Actual Day

On the day of the tournament get to the course at least one hour before tee-off time. This allows time for booking in, collecting the score card and any other relevant information and, most important of all, the warm-up, which has already been described in detail.

    Having done all the above, you still may not win the tournament, but at least you will have given yourself the best possible chance.

SECTION 3
Ailments and Injuries

Golf Injuries

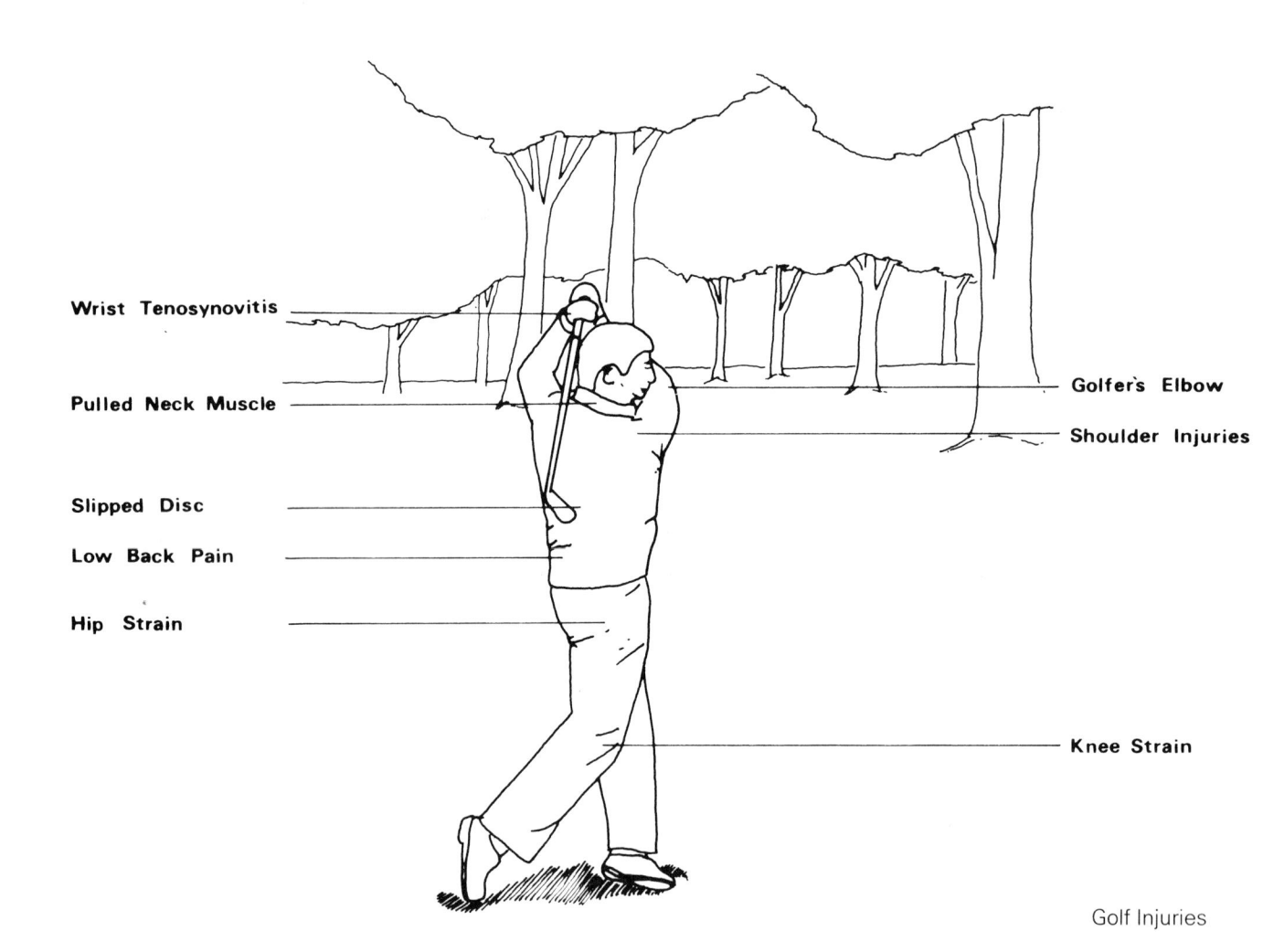

Introduction

Any physical exertion can cause a variety of aches and pains and this is as true with sport as with any other exercise. Each sport has its own spectrum of typical ailments and injuries, for the most part caused by sudden trauma or repeated wear and tear. Some can be prevented by having a good degree of prior fitness and training, but sportswomen and sportsmen are well advised to know something of the specific injuries that they could sustain when playing their chosen sport.

Specific Injuries Associated with Golf

Most golfing ailments are caused by the stresses, strains and frictions that occur in the swing. A long drive requires a clubhead speed of 100 mph to be reached in a fraction of a second. This means powerful and rapid action by most of the muscles and joints of the body, imparting a high degree of torque to the skeletal system. What is more, this action is repeated many times during a round. Not surprisingly, therefore, the predominant problems are over-use injuries, such as tendinitis, tenosynovitis and spondylosis, i.e. inflammation of tendons, tendon sheaths, and discs. Many of these problems can be avoided by minor modifications of swing technique, such as grip, stance and direction of take-away.

The illustration shows those injuries that may assail the golfer. The medical advice given below should enable him to recover as quickly as possible from such an injury and return to his game.

Neck

Pulled Muscle

Easily done with a poorly co-ordinated swing or inadequate warm-up, tearing a few fibres of one of the long muscles of the neck, or one of the trapezius muscles joining neck to shoulder. The result is a sharp neck-ache, ache at the back of the head, or shoulder, with severe twinges on active movement.

Treatment: rest. No neck twisting or heavy lifting. A soft surgical collar may be beneficial in the acute stage. After a few days of immobilisation, active exercise to strengthen the neck muscles should be started.

Strained Ligament

If the golfer's neck is rotated or bent backwards more then the ligaments linking the vertebrae may be strained, causing severe pain, even on passive movement.

Treatment: as for pulled muscle, except that recovery can be expected to take longer.

Slipped Disc

Not infrequent, especially in the older player. Usually part of chronic neck stiffness called cervical spondylosis. The disc loses its elasticity with advancing age, and a sudden lateral flexion or rotation, such as at the top of the backswing or follow-through, can burst an intervertebral disc and cause problems, particularly neuralgia down the arm.

Treatment: usually responds to rest, analgesics, perhaps a soft surgical collar. Physiotherapy or other hospital treatment may be needed. This injury incapacitates for weeks, if not months.

Shoulder

Tendonitis and Tenosynovitis

Because the shoulder joint has such a wide range of movement, the tendons of most of the muscles working the joint act like pulley-ropes running through grooves and around bony protuberances. Thus the tendons and their sheaths are subject to friction injury — tendonitis and tenosynovitis. The result is localised tenderness particularly of the leading shoulder during the swing.

Treatment: ice-packs in the first few hours, and analgesics. Then passive movements to avoid chronic stiffness — 'frozen shoulder'. After a few days, active exercises against resistance. Persistent shoulder pain that does not seem to be improving should be seen by a doctor.

Elbow

Golfer's Elbow (Epicondylitis)

This rather vague term refers to a sharp pain and tenderness felt where the forearm muscles join the boney prominences on either the inside (usually) or the outside of the elbow. The injury is akin to tennis elbow and is caused either by over-use of, or sudden jarring of, the tendinous insertions of the forearm muscles in the bone. Full wrist action becomes extremely painful, especially flexing the right wrist forwards (as in the down-swing of a right-handed player) and twisting it clockwise in the follow-through. Poor technique (stance, grip, action) is usually to blame, but so too is repeated undercutting (as with wet bunker-sand), playing from the rough, and playing after a long time away from golf.

Treatment: rest is the most important therapy; avoiding any action which tends to hurt the elbow. This means no golf (apart from putting practice) for a few weeks while the condition settles. If the onset was sudden and sharp, ice-packs may bring some immediate relief. But usually repeated trauma has made the condition chronic and warmth is more likely to help. Medical treatment (steroid injection) and physiotherapy may be necessary. But the injured tissue just needs time to heal, and the condition will recur if the forearm is not properly rested.

Wrist

Tenosynovitis

This is painful inflammation of a tendon sheath, commonly in the wrist. Tendons from the forearm muscles working the wrist and fingers pass through lubricated conduits or sheaths, and with over-use one or other of these can become inflamed, giving rise to a painful grating sensation in the wrist. In right-handed players it is the left wrist that is usually affected, especially at the base of the thumb (golfer's thumb). The top of the backswing, pre-impact down-swing and finish are the points where the trouble may arise. Minor changes in the action may avoid the condition.

Treatment: ice and analgesics in the acute phase when the tendon sheath is swollen like a sausage. Rest is most important, avoiding any action which tends to bring on the pain, which usually means no golf at all since grip is affected. Gentle, passive stretching movements of the wrist will help to prevent stiffness, and gentle wiggling of the thumb and fingers will keep them mobile. Once the tenderness has subsided, more active exercises can be started, including swing practice with a lighter iron.

Spine

Thoracic Pain

Felt between the shoulder blades, especially on twisting the back. Most spinal rotation takes place between its thoracic vertebrae, and the powerful torque forces of the golf-swing can strain intervertebral ligaments and muscles and 'slip' intervertebral discs.

Treatment: again the condition usually settles well with rest from the game (putting only). Avoid any action which twists the spine. If the condition does not improve within a fortnight or so, medical treatment should be sought.

Low Back Pain

Classic lumbago is an all too familiar complaint for golfers, by no means always caused by golfing. It can make almost any stroke an uncomfortable and sometimes impossible experience – even gentle putting. Bending the lumbar spine forwards, or to one side brings on the pain, usually felt across the lower back. Sciatica, an aching pain in the buttock and down the back of the leg, is caused by a 'slipped' lumbar disc. But most low back pain is the result of spondylosis, a chronic degeneration of the joints between the vertebrae, caused by years of spinal abuse – poor posture and strain – and the ageing process itself.

Treatment: with sudden severe backache, rest lying flat on a firm mattress for a day or two, or more if necessary. Be particularly careful to avoid any action which brings on the pain. Analgesics such as aspirin or paracetamol will help. In less severe, more chronic lumbago, back and trunk exercises can strengthen the spinal and abdominal musculature, providing a natural splint to the back. Swimming is a particularly beneficial form of exercise because it is non-weightbearing. Lumbar supports (corsets) are not a good idea because they soon weaken the back. Hospital treatment is sometimes necessary for frequent severe disc trouble and sciatica.

Hip

Hip Strain

Sometimes affects the left hip in right-handed players, especially at the bottom of the down-swing, follow-through and finish. Felt as an ache in the hip and thigh. Opening the left foot in the stance can prevent recurrence.

Treatment: rest for a week or two usually settles the condition.

Knee

Knee strain

In right-handed players this usually affects the inner side ligament of the right knee at the bottom of the down-swing, or the interior of the left knee-joint during follow-through.

Treatment: rest and warmth will help to heal the strained ligaments. Avoid any action which tends to bring on the pain, which means no golf except putting, perhaps for a few weeks.

Feet

Aching feet are not uncommon in golf, with all the walking, especially on the longer and hillier course. Correct footwear will help, with arch supports if necessary.

Environmental Problems

Heat and sun can be a problem in high summer. Light loose clothing will help, preferably a natural material such as cotton. A wide brimmed or peaked hat and sunshades will help to avoid eyestrain and headaches.

Exposure can be a real problem for winter golfers. Warm, dry and windproof clothing is essential. Gloves and a warm hat are important because much of the body heat is lost through the hands and head.

Thunderstorms are another threat. Lightning will seek the tallest object within a radius of a few hundred yards. If that object is a golfer . . . . Try not to get caught in thunderstorms, and if you do, seek low ground and avoid sitting under a tree.

General Ailments and Conditions

It is also useful for sportsmen and women to know something about the more general ailments and conditions that are difficult to avoid, whatever their chosen sport.

Skin and Subcutaneous Tissue

The skin and subcutaneous tissues are most vulnerable to friction and impact.

Blisters

These are caused by repeated friction of unprotected skin in which the outer layer of skin (epidermis) is separated from the inner layer (dermis) by inflammatory tissue fluid – or occasionally blood (the blood blister).

Treatment: if the blister is not likely to cause trouble it can be left alone to settle, but if in danger of being rubbed, cover it with a piece of sticking plaster.

Usually, however, it is threatening to burst and this is the moment when infection can occur. On these occasions it is best to lance it under sterile conditions. First cleanse the skin thoroughly with antiseptic. Then sterilise a needle in a flame for a few seconds and holding it parallel to the skin puncture the edge of the blister (*do not remove the loose skin*). Gently dab dry and squeeze to remove the fluid, then cover with a porous sticking plaster.

Prevention: you can prevent blisters by using sticking plaster to cover any rubbing point that is beginning to feel sore. The first indications of a blister are likely to be a soreness and reddening of the area.

Abrasions (Grazes)

Abrasions are due to the scuffing away of the epidermis completely.

Treatment: cleanse under a running tap to wash away dirt or grit (or use an antiseptic solution). When thoroughly clean, allow wound to dry, or dry by dabbing with a sterile gauze, and cover with a porous dressing.

Minor Cuts

Minor cuts should be treated similarly and covered with a sticking plaster. For more severe lacerations and bleeding see First Aid, p. 65.

Deep, Penetrating Wounds

Deep, penetrating wounds, such as caused by a nail spiking the foot, may need a tetanus injection. If the wound has been made by an object which you suspect as being infected, you are advised as a matter of course to have a precautionary tetanus injection.

Bruises (Contusions)

Bruises are areas of skin and subcutaneous tissue in which the tiny capillaries are damaged by a sudden blow. (The colouring of a bruise is due to blood oozing into the tissue.)

Treatment: an ice-pack (ice cubes in a towel — it is a mistake to apply ice direct to the skin [see illustration]) applied as soon as possible to the bruise will help to reduce the colouring and swelling. However, if the blow was severe, bruising may mask a fracture of the underlying bone and an X-ray is advisable.

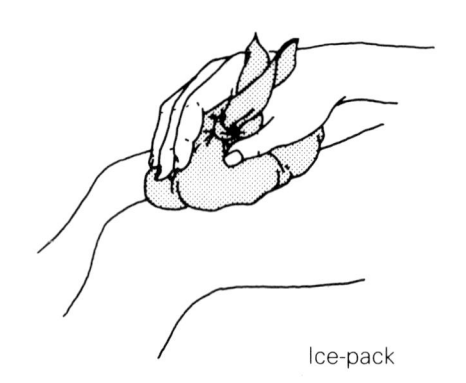

Ice-pack

Muscle Injuries

These are usually due to repeated over-use or sudden over-stretching of untuned muscles. Most can be prevented by adequate fitness and training, and the all-important warm-up before strenuous exercise.

Muscle Aches (Muscle Soreness, Stiffness)

Muscle aches are caused by imposing unaccustomed exercise on groups of untrained muscles.

When muscles are worked hard they will swell with tissue fluid from the capillaries surrounding the muscle fibres. The fluid bathes the fibres and carries away irritant waste products of muscle contraction. *Untrained* muscles remain swollen with fluid long after exercise has stopped and this causes pain and stiffness which can take place as much as 12-24 hours afterwards, although usually much sooner.

Treatment: muscle aches can be relieved by warmth to increase the blood flow (e.g. a hot bath, shower, hot-water bottle or embrocation.) Gentle massage and kneading the affected muscle may also help, especially while under hot water.

Muscle Spasm (Cramp)

Cramp is a sudden involuntary contraction of a muscle — classically the calf — causing temporary but crippling pain. It usually results from over-exertion, poor co-ordination or extreme cold — when the muscles tense — or extreme heat — when excessive sweating can lead to salt depletion.

Treatment: the most effective way to deal with cramp is to stretch the knotted muscle, in order to pull it out of spasm, and then massage it along its length.

Prevention: in hot weather add a pinch or two of salt to a fruit drink.

Stitch

A stitch is a spasm or cramp of a muscle in the side of the trunk, usually felt between or below the lower ribs.

Treatment: it can be eased by taking a deep breath in and holding it. Other techniques are to flex the trunk to the side away from the stitch or push the fingers deep into the side and bend forward.

Prevention: avoid exertion within two hours of a heavy meal.

Muscle Pulls or Tears

Muscle pulls or tears are the most common form of muscle injury and are caused by a muscle suddenly becoming over-stretched and rupturing some of the fibres. This causes intense pain, swelling and loss of function. A pulled muscle is often the result of a sudden awkward or unexpected movement in sport – a twist, or sudden stop or turn.

Treatment: stop immediately, for it is essential to rest the injured muscle as soon as possible (it would be agony to use it anyway). Apply an ice-pack and strap the pack to the injured muscle with a firm bandage in order to apply compression. If possible, elevate the injured part to help drain away inflammatory fluid.

This routine is the classic prescription for soft-tissue injuries and is sometimes given the shorthand name of R-I-C-E. (i.e. rest – ice – compression – elevation).

After 48 hours start gentle mobilisation exercises: flex the injured part back and forwards *gently*, taking care to avoid painful movement. It may also be useful to try alternate hot and cold treatments (hot towels/ice-packs alternating every 20-30 minutes). After a few days' passive stretching, you can begin active exercise, building up gradually to full activity in a few weeks.

Prevention: to avoid pulled or torn muscles it is essential to carry out a thorough warm-up before exercise (*see p. 27*).

Tendons

These are the tough fibrous strands on which muscles tug to flex or extend joints. Tendons are sometimes strained, partially torn or completely ruptured.

Symptoms: these range from pain and swelling to total loss of function.

Treatment: for lesser injuries the R-I-C-E routine (*see above*) should be started immediately; the cold compress reduces inflammation and damage. If the tendon is ruptured (and the muscles then bunch into a knot or spasm), medical attention should be sought.

Tendon Sheath

In some sports, over-use of a particular joint can lead to an irritation of the tendon sheath or lining. The resulting inflammation is called *tenosynovitis* (tendonitis) and causes shooting pain when the joint is moved.

Tendinous Insertions

Additionally, where the bulk of a muscle is anchored to a bone there are short tendinous insertions. These can sometimes be torn, usually when movement is suddenly blocked and the muscle is jarred (e.g. a squash player hitting the wall, a football player mis-kicking). The shin and elbow are classic sites of such tendinous insertions. When torn, this leads to 'shin splints' for the former and 'tennis elbow' for the latter.

Treatment: applying an ice-pack may give relief, but rest is the only cure. Your doctor may recommend other treatments and these may alleviate the symptoms temporarily, but the trouble will return unless the limb is rested because tendons are very slow to heal.

Sprains

Sprain is the term used to describe a partially torn ligament, which is a fibrous strap binding the bones of a joint together.

If a ligament tears, the joint cannot be moved without pain and soon swells. Classic sites are the ankle, the knee and the wrist.

Treatment: immediate course of action is the R-I-C-E routine. Rest is crucial; continued use of the joint will lead to chronic disability.

Bone Injuries (see First Aid, p. 69)

Hot-weather Ailments

Heat Exhaustion

Excessive sweating can lead to loss of essential water and salts. Usually, thirst provides a strong incentive to drink to replace the water, but not the salt. Salt depletion causes the victim to feel dizzy and faint, probably with a headache. It may also bring cramp (see p. 62). If salt is not replaced soon this can lead to the highly dangerous heat stroke (see First Aid, p. 70).

Prevention: add an extra pinch or two of salt to your food in hot weather before exercise.

Prickly Heat

Prickly heat is another hot-weather condition. It is caused by high humidity making the skin waterlogged, thus blocking the sweat glands and causing irritation.

Prevention: wear light, loose cotton-type clothing and try to restrict exertion to the cooler times of the day.

Sunburn

Prevention: use a suitable sunscreen to protect exposed parts.

Treatment: sunburn can be relieved with cool water or calamine lotion.

Cold-weather Ailments

Physical activity in cold weather usually keeps you warm, but the extremities – ears, nose, fingers and toes – can be affected by cold, when they will turn white and feel numb. In extreme conditions they can even become frostbitten. So wear suitable headgear, gloves and extra socks in very cold weather.

Also, in these conditions, muscles tend to tense up. So to avoid injury it is important to carry out a thorough warm-up routine before exertion (*see p. 27*).

Prolonged exposure to severe cold, especially if soaked to the skin, can lead to the potentially fatal hypothermia.

First Aid for Sports

There are a number of common and not-so-common, sporting emergencies. This section discusses how to deal with them until medical help arrives. Most First Aid is simple practical common sense. But some techniques – in particular mouth-to-mouth respiration and cardiac massage – can really only be learned properly from a qualified instructor.

Bleeding

Severe bleeding is usually from a deep cut (laceration), torn flesh (avulsion) or penetrating wound.

Symptoms: spurting, bright-red blood indicates that an artery has been severed and the flow must be stopped *immediately*. Oozing darker blood from the veins indicates that the situation is not so urgent but the blood flow should be stopped as soon as possible.

Treatment: with both types of blood flow the treatment is essentially the same. With a clean handkerchief, or pad of absorbent material, or even your bare hands, hold together the edges of the wound and press hard to stop bleeding.

Maintaining the pressure, lay the casualty down and raise the injured part above the level of the heart, if possible. If blood seeps through the pad put another on top. *Do not release the pressure on the wound.*

Reassure the casualty and send for medical assistance, but do not leave the casualty alone for more than a minute or two, and only if you have bound the pressure pad in place.

Gaping wounds will usually need stitches. Deep wounds, especially those caused by a dirty or muddy object, may call for an anti-tetanus injection.

Nosebleed

Treatment: pinch the soft part of the nose for 10-15 minutes, or until bleeding stops. Do not swallow blood but spit it out into a cup or basin. Do not blow or pick the nose and try to avoid sneezing for the next 12 hours. An ice-pack over the nose will also prove beneficial.

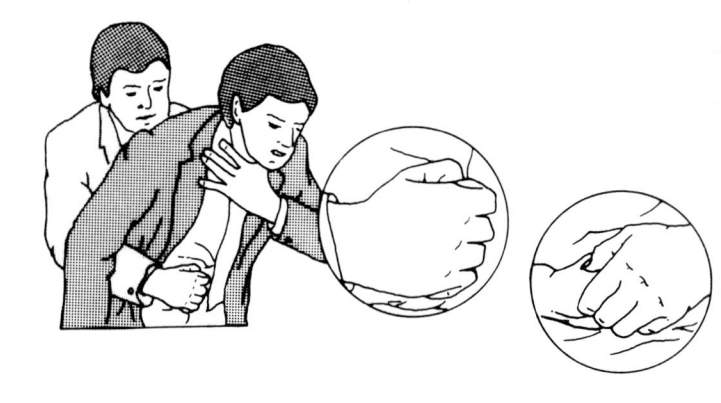

Heimlich Manoeuvre. Stand behind the casualty. Put your arm around his waist making a fist with one hand, clasping it with the other, and with thumbs resting just above his navel. Make three or four sharp pulls diagonally upwards towards you.

Breathing Difficulty

Choking

Choking is unusual in sports, but may occur if someone inhales chewing gum or a false tooth. A blocked windpipe makes the person struggle for breath and the lips turn blue.

Treatment: get the casualty to bend forward and give him several sharp slaps between the shoulder blades to help dislodge the blockage. If this doesn't work, try the Heimlich Manoeuvre (*see illustrations*). If you cannot clear the blockage quickly, send for urgent medical help; an emergency tracheotomy may be necessary.

Similarly, call for urgent medical help if someone is choking due to a sharp blow to the throat which has caused internal swelling of the windpipe, or if someone has a severe attack of asthma.

Stopped Breathing

If a person loses consciousness, perhaps after a blow to the head, or a faint, they may stop breathing and start to go purplish-blue. This may simply be because the tongue has fallen against the back of the throat and blocked the windpipe.

Treatment: turn the person face down so that the tongue can fall forwards. If he takes a long breath in and continues to breathe, keep him in this face down 'recovery' position (sometimes called the 'coma' position) and send for medical help (*see illustration*).

If no breath follows, then turn him face up again and start mouth-to-mouth respiration (the 'kiss of life') (*see illustrations*).

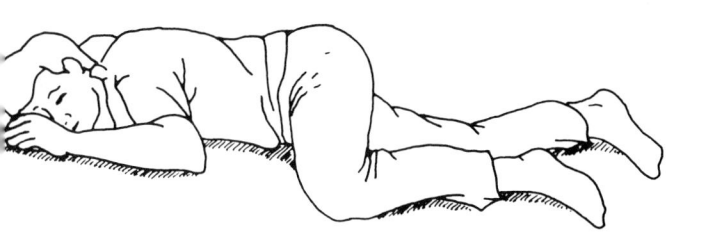

The recovery, or coma position

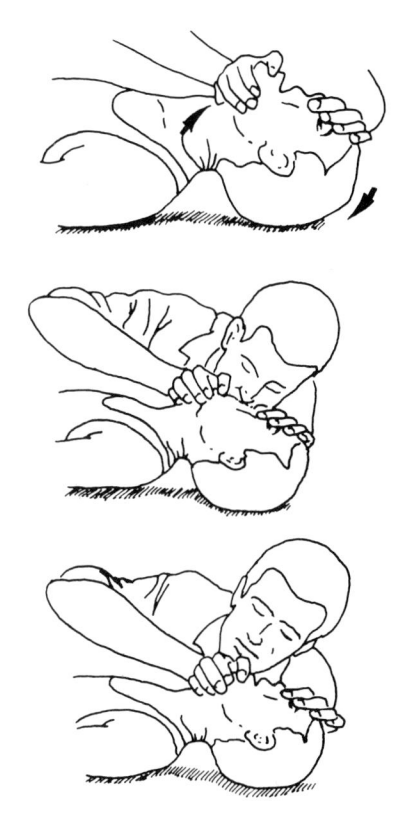

Mouth-to-mouth artificial respiration

Mouth-to-mouth Respiration: with one hand pinch his nostrils shut and push his forehead back so that his chin juts upwards. With the other hand hold his jaw open and lift it away from his neck to pull the tongue off the back of the throat. Now take a deep breath and, sealing your lips round the casualty's mouth, blow air into his lungs, watching to see his chest rise as you do so. Then remove your mouth and watch his chest fall again. Do this four times and then check the pulse (*see p.9*). If the heart is beating, continue mouth-to-mouth at the rate of 16-18 breaths a minute, checking the pulse every minute or so. If you are doing the job properly the casualty's lips and tongue should become a healthy-looking pink. Keep the respiration going until help arrives or until the casualty starts to breathe spontaneously, in which case turn him face down into the recovery position (*see illustration*).

If you cannot feel his pulse, or he remains purple despite several good respirations, then his heart has stopped beating, and you must start cardiac massage immediately (*see p.86*).

Heart Problems

Heart Attack

This is a not uncommon misfortune that may befall the unfit (usually men) who suddenly over-exert themselves. Most people survive their first heart attack, but smokers have double the risk of dying.

Symptoms: the classic symptom of a heart attack is a heavy vice-like pain in the chest — like severe indigestion – which may spread to the arms or jaw. The victim usually feels faint and sick.

Treatment: if you suspect a heart attack, send someone for an ambulance, but do not leave the victim alone.

If he remains conscious, rest and reassurance are the most important things. Get him in a half-sitting position with his shoulders propped on a rolled up coat or blanket (*see illustration*). Loosen his clothing and cover him with a coat or towel. Do *not* give him anything by mouth, not even brandy or aspirin. Stay with him until help arrives.

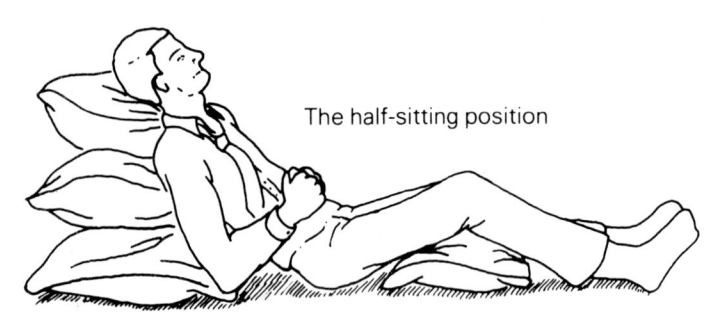

The half-sitting position

If he loses consciousness and stops breathing suspect cardiac arrest (stopped heart) which calls for immediate cardiac massage, and mouth-to-mouth respiration.

Stopped Heart (Cardiac Arrest)

This is to be suspected if a person collapses unconscious and stops breathing. The victim will probably go an ashen colour with purple lips and tongue. The cause may be a heart attack or severe attack following haemorrhage or crush injury.

Treatment: feel for the casualty's pulse. Put two fingers at *one side* of his Adam's apple and press firmly. If you cannot feel pulsations, try the other side. Look at the pupils of his eyes. No pulse and wide fixed pupils spells cardiac arrest. Start cardiac massage immediately. *This is not to be attempted if the heart is beating* (*see illustrations*).

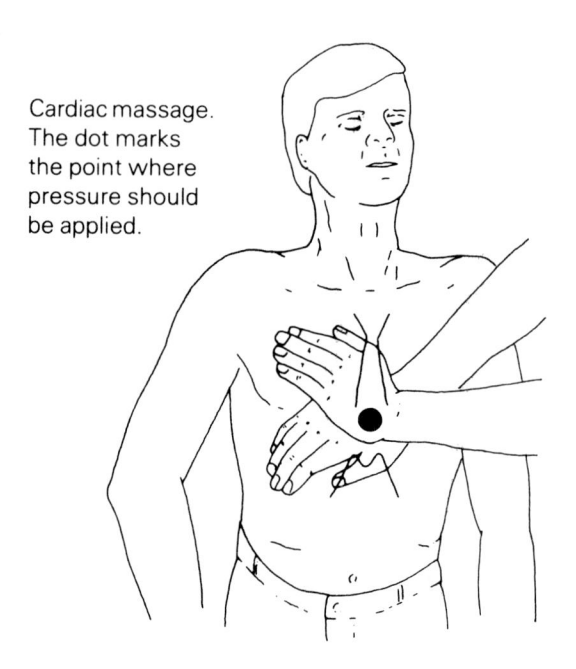

Cardiac massage. The dot marks the point where pressure should be applied.

Cardiac Massage: lay the person on his back on firm ground. Quickly clear his mouth of any vomit or blood clot with a sweep or two of your finger. Give four breaths of mouth-to-mouth respiration as above. This may be enough to stimulate the heart into action, so quickly check the heart again.

If there is still no pulse, kneel alongside the casualty. Put the heel of one hand on the lower half of his breast-bone in the midline, just above the V-shaped notch made by the ribs. Cover this hand with the heel of the other. Now keeping your arms straight, push down on your hands, moving his breastbone down about 6.25 cm (1½ in.) and release. Repeat this pressure about 80 times a minute. Count to yourself: one pressure, two pressure, three pressure . . . etc. After 15 pressures, give two more respirations, and then continue pressures. Keep going with 15 pressures, 2 respirations etc. Every few minutes stop to check the pulse. If you feel one, stop cardiac massage but continue respirations. If spontaneous breathing starts, put him in the recovery position (*see illustration*). Do not abandon your efforts until help arrives.

Unconsciousness

Usually caused by a blow to the head, but sometimes due to a diabetic coma, epileptic fit or heart attack (*see above*).

The most important action is to check for breathing. If the casualty is not breathing, mouth-to-mouth respiration must be started immediately.

If the casualty is unconscious but still breathing, turn him face down into the 'recovery' or 'coma' position (*see p. 68*). This allows the tongue to fall forwards away from the back of the throat where it would block the windpipe.

Send for immediate medical help, but do not leave the casualty unattended, check his breathing every few minutes.

Head Injury

This can range from a cut scalp to a fractured skull, but usually refers to a blow on the head sufficient to knock out the victim for seconds or minutes.

Concussion

The likely consequence is concussion, a temporary disorientation causd by jarring the brain. This may be accompanied by giddiness and memory loss.

Contusion (Bruising)

More serious is brain contusion, which leaves a scar in the brain substance and usually causes some permanent loss of memory and intellectual capacity (i.e. 'punch-drunk').

Compression

The most serious and life-threatening result is compression: an inter-cranial haemorrhage (bleeding inside the skull). The build-up of pressure can rapidly lead to loss of consciousness and death, unless the pressure is released by emergency surgery. Compression can occur up to 48 hours after injury.

Symptoms: drowsiness, confusion, dilation of one or both pupils of the eye.

Treatment: any person knocked out by a head injury should be made to lie quietly and be looked at every half hour or so to check the level of consciousness.

If you observe any of the symptoms of compression listed above, get the victim to hospital immediately.

Facial Injury

Black Eye

Usually looks far worse than it is. As soon as you can, apply an ice-pack or cold compress to prevent or reduce the swelling. It is wise to have the eye checked by a doctor to make sure that vision is not impared.

Broken Nose

Usually accompanied by bleeding, swelling and deformed appearance. Bleeding should be stopped as described above (*p. 67*). Sometimes the nose can be straightened immediately, but usually it is best to put on an ice-pack or cold compress and get the casualty to hospital.

Broken cheekbones and broken jaws should also be covered with an ice-pack to reduce swelling and the casualty taken to hospital.

Fractures and Dislocations

Broken bones and disrupted joints are usually obvious, especially in the more serious cases. Sometimes, however, swelling and bruising can mask such injuries, e.g. stress fracture of the foot.

Treatment: it is important not to try to bear weight on a fracture or dislocation as this could damage a nerve or blood vessel. It is also important not to try to straighten the injury, unless you know precisely what you are doing, for you could cause even more damage.

The most useful thing to do is to keep the injured part as immobile as possible – use splints, slings or stretchers as necessary. The casualty should be taken to hospital where the injury can be X-rayed and the deformity reduced under medical supervision, with an anaesthetic if necessary.

Environmental Emergencies

Heat Stroke

This is a very serious condition and can occur after prolonged exertion in a very hot or humid environment. It is caused by the body's temperature-regulating system breaking down and, as a result, the temperature rises alarmingly.

Symptoms: the victim has a hot dry skin, rapid pulse and looks flushed. Confusion and coma can follow rapidly.

Treatment: *medical attention is urgent.* The important thing is to *cool* the victim down as quickly as possible with water or ice, and then to keep him fanned to induce cooling.

Frostbite

This is also potentially serious. The body is composed of 70 per cent water and if ice-crystals form in human tissue it is destroyed.

Treatment: numbed and frozen extremities should be got into the warm as soon as possible and held against warm skin. *Do not apply direct heat and do not rub the frozen part* – you might literally rub the flesh away. Do not stand or walk on frozen toes or feet, but rest with the feet up.

Index

Abdomen 20
Advice for Aspiring Champions 52-4
Aerobics 10
Arms and Shoulders 14, 17, 18, 19

Balanced Fitness 11
Blisters 61
Body Suppleness Exercises 45
Breathing Difficulties 67-8
Bruises 62
Building up Strength 40

Cardiac Arrest 68
Chair Squat 44
Check your Equipment 54
Circuit Training 25-7, 47
Cold-weather Ailments 65, 71
Compression 69
Concussion 69
Correct Equipment 49-52
Cuts 62

Dislocation 71
Dynamics 10

Elements of Fitness 9
Environmental Emergencies 70
Environmental Problems 60
Exercise Sessions 11-27

Facial Injuries 70
Feel of the Swing, The 38-9
Fingertip Press-ups 19, 43
First Aid 65-71

Fit for Sport 7
Fitness Ethic, The 6
Fitness Testing 7
Fluid Turning 44
Fractures 70
Frostbite 71

Golf, Specific Injuries 57-61
Golfer's Elbow 60
Grips 51

Hamstring 12
Head Injuries 69
Heart 67-8
Heat Stroke 71
Hip Strain 12
Hooking 35

Isometrics 10

Jogging 25

Knees 16, 60

Leg Raise 44
Legs 16, 21-4
Long Putts 40
Low Back Pain 59

Muscle Aches 64
Muscle Pulls or Tears 63-4

Neck 13, 45
Nosebleed 66

One-handed Swing 41

Physical Demands of Golf, The 34
Posture 37-8
Pulse Rate Test 9
Putting 39

Recovery Shots 39
Repairing the Damage 46

Setting up the Ball 35-9
Shins 24
Shoulders 13, 17, 18
Short Putts 29
Sprains 64
Stance and Alignment 37
Strength Exercises 17-25
Strengthening Legs 43
Suppleness Exercises 11-16, 45-6

Tendonitis 59
Tenosynovitis 59
Thighs 15, 21
Tyre Exercise 59

Unconsciousness 69
Upper Body Garments 50
Upper Legs 16

Warming-up and Warming-down 27-8
Warming-up before a Round 48-9
Weight and Fitness 29
Wet-weather Clothing 50
Wrists and Arms 19